ORDINARY
HEAVEN

EXPLORING SPIRITUAL DIRECTION
AND THE JOURNEY OF HUMAN LIFE

Philip Carter is passionate about spiritual direction and is one of the fathers of spiritual direction in Australia. The book is a testament to his passion and commitment to craft a theological and experiential understanding of spiritual direction. In Philip's unique style, he weaves together a lifetime of experience and reflection with pearls of wisdom from poets, mystics and spiritual writers, all with an Australian flavour. This book is a must read for those engaged on the spiritual journey.

—Sue Dunbar, Director of Barnabas Ministries Inc.

Philip Carter's book is a lifetime of accumulated richness in one place. For this reason, readers will want to pause and savour the wisdom as they make their way through each chapter. In this collection, Philip brings together threads of personal knowledge and anecdotes with inspiring quotes and theology from the breadth of tradition in ways that will illumine both givers and receivers of spiritual direction. Regardless of one's starting point—new explorer, seasoned practitioner or student in formation—Philip's book will be a gift to unpack, return to and share with others.

—Christine Gilbert, Editor of Coolamon, journal of the Australian Network for Spiritual Direction (ANSD)

Philip Carter writes in a way that awakens me to my sacredness as a human person and to the essential beauty of a calling to spiritual direction in the Christian tradition. This book is much more than many wise and practical insights for spiritual directors and those seeking spiritual companionship. It is a gift of love and an invitation to Holy encounter. Carter offers this treasure with an earthy grace, drawing on his long experience of embodying a listening presence. What a hopeful and vital offering for our times.

—Dr. Rachael Litchfield, Ecumenical Spiritual Directors Association, South Australia

As all good spiritual directors do, Philip Carter invites us into the space and holds it for us, distilling the wisdom of others with that of his own to remind us of the life-changing potential of this ministry. Carter's book is right up there with Guenther's classic "Holy Listening"—a must for all spiritual directors and directors-in-formation. Without a doubt, this book is one for the required reading list!

—Sally Jones, GDSD, M. Min, Program Director, Listen into Life: Residential Program in Spiritual Direction, Chairperson of the Australian Ecumenical Council for Spiritual Direction

Wise, sensitive, discerning, heartfelt, deeply informative—this is the book we have been waiting for. The spiritual direction community is in good hands with this offering from Philip Carter.

—Cath Connelly, Living Well Centre Co-Director, Spiritual Director and retreat leader

Philip Carter's book should be read by students commencing their formation in spiritual direction, again as they finish their training, and then kept on their bookshelf for easy access. Speaking from years of experience, Carter provides theological underpinning for the practice of spiritual direction. Using the voices of a variety of writers and drawing on his own personal experiences as a spiritual director, this accessible book outlines the what, how, and why of spiritual direction practice. Whether exploring a particular topic, such as discernment or relationality, or seeking a thorough and grounded overview of the ministry, Carter's book will benefit seasoned spiritual directors and those in their early formation alike.

—Cathie Lambert, Director, The Dayspring Community

This book distills the heart of the vocation of spiritual direction in the Christian tradition - theologically deep, spiritually attuned and lovingly oriented to the transfiguration of humanity. Each paragraph, each sentence, calls to be read slowly and savoured as in lectio divina. This is a book for spiritual directors and spiritual seekers which speaks from and points to the mystery in which we are sourced, and which beckons us infinitely on. A treasure.

—Sarah Bachelard, Author of Experiencing God in a Time of Crisis and Resurrection and Moral Imagination

Spiritual direction books abound, but here Philip Carter communicates a prism of possibilities, and paints vividly the synergy between poetry and spiritual direction. With the sagacity that emerges from deep experience, Carter draws on his learnings from those he has accompanied, and authors who have accompanied him, thus inviting us to venture into a full-orbed mystagogy of the ministry of spiritual direction. This is a book we have been waiting for!

—Sally Longley, Author of Conversations with Silence: Rosetta Stone of the Soul

By listening with wholehearted and pure attention, seeking to discern what the Spirit is offering or calling forth in the life of the directee, the spiritual director makes an act of contemplative prayer. Philip Carter's new book is a wonderfully rich and insightful exploration of how spiritual direction can be a place of transfiguration, and a place of discovering the living water of the Spirit.

—Roland Ashby, Spiritual Director, author, and coordinator of the World Community for Christian Meditation, Victoria

Philip writes in a way that makes this book very easy to read as it has a logical structure that flows with wonderful clarity and warmth. His style of writing embraces key concepts of spiritual direction while allowing the words to draw the reader to engage at heart level, encouraging us to dive deeper and respond to the grace of deep listening. He beautifully weaves reflections and contributions from many respected writers with both traditional and contemporary theological views and blends these with the richness of his own spiritual journey and his experience of accompanying others. The result is creative and balanced.

Philip's wisdom and reverence for the art of spiritual direction and its importance in our contemporary world invites an expanding vision of the spaciousness and sacredness of the spiritual direction relationship, where he affirms the holiness and sacredness of each encounter. I particularly resonated with Philip's emphasis on the Holy Place of Transfiguration, shining light on the practice of spiritual direction, quoting his words, "The transfiguration provides an astonishingly illuminating lens through which to see both the inner dynamic and charism of spiritual direction." When I finished reading I felt drawn in to seek and experience more. This a highly recommended and nourishing read for both beginners and those experienced in the ministry of spiritual direction.

—Wayne Brabin, Ignatian Heart Spirituality Ministry

ORDINARY HEAVEN

EXPLORING SPIRITUAL DIRECTION AND THE JOURNEY OF HUMAN LIFE

PHILIP CARTER

2024

SDI PRESS
SEATTLE, WASHINGTON, USA

Published by SDI Press, a division of Spiritual Directors International, 3800 Aurora Ave N, Suite 120, Seattle, WA 98103, USA.

www.sdicompanions.org
ISBN: 978-1-950309-07-8

Cover design: Matt Whitney

Book layout: Ann Lancaster

TABLE OF CONTENTS

ACKNOWLEDGEMENTS

All that is written here, was done so on the traditional land of Australia's First Nation people—the Kaurna people. I pay my respects to the traditional people of this land, past, present and to come. I express gratitude in the sharing of this land, sorrow for the personal, spiritual, and cultural costs of that sharing, and hope that we may walk together in harmony, in the spirit of Reconciliation.

My personal journey into the ministry of spiritual direction began in earnest when I noticed I was being drawn by people's requests to talk with me about their spiritual life. In 1984 I saw a notice for a spiritual direction formation program in Wollaston College, Perth. Speaking to Keith Rayner, the then Archbishop of Adelaide, I was encouraged to apply. From 1984-1986 I attended the August program of that formation course, and it set me on a path ending in my appointment in a Ministry in Spirituality for the Diocese of Adelaide based at the Diocesan Retreat House. The Sisters of the Community of the Holy Name had been running the Retreat House for many years, and after 18 months there my ministry included running the Retreat centre. In 1997 I left the Retreat House and the Diocesan Ministry in Spirituality, and opened the Julian Centre, an ecumenical, independent spirituality centre, just outside the CBD of the City of Adelaide. I am grateful to Jonathan Wells for his friendship, support and encouragement over many years, to Maxine Smith, who was my Administrative Assistant for 13 years at the Centre, and to Faye Lindsay, who helped with reception at the Centre each Friday.

***

The formation program at Wollaston College ran for 3 weeks every August for 3 years, and the teaching staff included both local and international people. One year the international guest was Bishop

1

Trevor Huddleston, acting as Chaplain to the course, who was well known as a champion in the fight against Apartheid in South Africa. It's been said that Trevor Huddleston lived from the inside out: his actions emanated out of a sustained way of seeing things, a controlling theological vision, which led him to become a champion of social justice. Such a vision acts as an interpretative lens, allowing a person to live congruently, such that one's life becomes a natural embodiment of that vision. Trevor Huddleston, following Jesus of Nazareth, helped me see that the true miracle of spiritual direction is the manner, or the way in which we are with others. He also helped me realize that while so much of the spiritual direction relationship is between two people, with the focus on the personal and interpersonal circumstances and issues of the directee, it is not conducted as if in a vacuum, but always situated within the wider context of their social, national and international worlds.

***

While I have long been committed to the ongoing professional skills and development of spiritual directors, what is crucial, I believe, is the personal vocation of the spiritual director, what Margaret Guenther called the "amateur status" of spiritual directors, for the amateur is the one who "loves the art that she serves". Of course, spiritual direction requires skills, which are taught and learned: but art is a gift. The amateur is marked by a humility and patience, waiting for others to name her gift. (Guenther, 1). Thomas Merton understood that our "right place" is poverty of spirit, knowing who we really are before God. In words that are a wonderful expression of the personal vocation of the spiritual director Merton writes in *Learning to Love*: "My fall into inconsistency was nothing but the revelation of what I am.... I am thrown into contradiction: to realize it is mercy, to accept it is love, to help others do the same is compassion" (Merton, 106,355).

***

George Trippe, Director of Wollaston College at the time, had a background in counselling and therapy, and in one of the years of the course he invited Jack Dominian, a Senior Consultant Psychiatrist at the Central Middlesex Hospital, and a well-known author, who recognized the importance of the interface between psychology and Christianity. Up until this time, my main preoccupation in my reading had been acquainting myself with the Christian spiritual tradition, and it was this "awareness of dynamic psychology [as] an invaluable tool in understanding not only the mechanisms of human behaviour but the depths of Christian spirituality" that I was particularly hungry for (Dominian, x).

***

One memorable workshop which I attended in the early 1990's, was a workshop conducted by Gerard W, Hughes. S.J. I had long been drawn to Gerard Hughes, and his writing, not least *The God of Surprises*, which included his refreshing phrase, "God is a beckoning word." This is indeed the God of surprises, calling us out of and beyond ourselves, and always creating anew. He was clear that "Nothing so masks the face of God as religion." I distinctly remember in the workshop when he said that if "God" gets in the way for the person coming for spiritual direction, then use the language of life. He suggests in *God of Surprises* writing your own obituary—the one in your wildest dreams you would love to have—which opens up the possibility for us to get in touch with our inner life, and an indication of what we really want. The choice is stark, between "Events which lead to life" and "Events which deaden me" (Hughes, 31 and 9). As the Book of Deuteronomy puts it: "I have set before you life and death.... Choose life." (Dt. 30,19)

***

Another memorable workshop in 1991, in a Conference organized by the Australian Network for Spiritual Direction (ANSD), was conducted by the well-known Australian spiritual director, Brian Gallagher, MSC. In his keynote lecture entitled "Spiritual Direction and the Human Experience of God," he suggested that spiritual directors "are called to live in two worlds; the world of our everyday ordinariness, permeated and seasoned by the Spirit, and the world also of the Spirit, that we touch only by transcending our everyday ordinariness." This incarnational celebration of being human struck me then as utterly central to the spiritual director's vocation. He ended his talk by saying that we are utterly dependent on God's mercy and love. Far from talking about my call, my spirituality, my ministry, he said that, as Thomas Merton said in Contemplative Prayer, we need the hell of mercy, the hell of being purified of all self-sufficiency and self-complacency....all illusions of "being good at the job," of "having it all together," of "being spiritual directors" (Merton, 102).

***

One person, a woman of the 14th century, who has had an abiding and deep influence on me is of course, Julian of Norwich. I love her because she is grounded and earthed, because she wrestles with questions around faith and meaning, because she is both a realist and a woman of hope. I remember Margaret Guenther, in a workshop I invited her to run in Adelaide, where she talked of those words of God Julian makes so much of: "All will be well, and all will be well, and every kind of thing will be well" (Julian, 27). Her very graphic and poignant commentary was to think of the women and children in cattle trucks on their way to Auschwitz to certain death. She pictured mothers holding their little children in their arms and saying to them, "It's going to be alright. It's going to be alright." This is surely a truth that can only be forged in the furnace of love. For Julian love is our Lord's meaning, but it is also our meaning as well.

***

One of the striking things about my journey has been the community of spiritual directors that I have been enfolded in. After my formation course in Wollaston College, I joined the local Adelaide Catholic Spiritual Directors' Association with my colleague and friend Ann Siddall, and we worked with that group and saw it become the Ecumenical Spiritual Directors Association of South Australia (ESDA). For many years I was a part of a Supervision group linked to ESDA. In 1989, together with several others, I became a founding member of the Australian Network for Spiritual Direction (ANSD), and for a time was its President. Between 2006 and 2009 I was the Inaugural President of the Australian Ecumenical Council for Spiritual Direction. In July 2006 I attended and completed the Internship in the art of supervision of spiritual directors at the Mercy Center in Burlingame, California. The camaraderie and support that I encountered through all these groups is incalculable. I am grateful to Frances MacKay and John Foulcher, editors of the Australian spirituality journal Eremos, for their encouragement of my writing.

I must also mention my membership of Spiritual Directors International (SDI), and the publication of its journal *Presence*, which I have received since its beginning, and my thanks to Nick Wagner, SeiFu Anil Singh-Molares, Matt Whitney, and Seicho Sydney Roth for their encouragement and editorial help over the years.

In Adelaide, Ann Siddall and I worked with an ecumenical team, and offered four Formation programs for aspiring spiritual directors, the first two programs with John Helm and Henry Palenschus, and the second two programs with Gary Stuckey and Russell Bartlett. With my colleague and friend John Stewart, the Director of the Living Well Centre in Melbourne, we offered a Formation Program in Brisbane over 4 years. With another colleague and friend, Sue Dunbar, Director of Barnabas Ministries in Canberra, I offered workshops and lectures in formation programs which Barnabas Ministries ran in both Kincumber and Canberra.

I also must mention the very many people who came to me over those years for spiritual direction. I cannot begin to say how they gifted me over the years, taught me about the human condition, opened me up towards the generosity of God, and offered me on a daily basis, encounters of mystery and depth, laughter and sadness, questions and invitations which, in my stumbling way, helped me to grow as a person and as a spiritual director. They encouraged me to see that faith is above all openness towards everything that is, that love is at the heart of the spiritual direction relationship, and that hope is not optimism, but a way of living in this world, knowing, not how things will turn out so much as knowing that whatever happens it has meaning and can give us the courage to take the next step.

Finally, I cannot end with out mentioning Helen—who has been supportive of this ministry over many years—and our 3 adult daughters. I look back and realize how often I have been away from home, conducting several retreats every year through the Retreat House and the Julian Centre, and ten or so visits to Malaysia over 20 years. I am extremely grateful for their support.

Philip Carter
January 2024

FOREWORD

Philip Carter, an Anglican priest hailing from Australia, has served in the ministry of spiritual direction for 40 years. Often referred to as the "land down under" in reference to Australia's geographical position south of the equator, in contrast, I would call this an "up and above" book. In the pages that follow, Carter inspires and challenges us to look at the ministry of spiritual direction as a ministry of connection—to self, to others, to the earth, and to the Sacred.

A scholarly resource, the references cited here could easily provide the reader with cache of treasured resources that span poetry, theology, philosophy and beyond. Philip Carter's spiritual influences are not bound by faith tradition; he pulls at the threads that connect all spiritual living. At the same time, the stories that are shared here from his extensive personal experience in spiritual direction, are practical, genuine, and relatable.

In describing the ministry of spiritual direction as conversation, Carter invites directors to notice and attend to how they are present to another during the meeting. He reflects deeply around the need to be a welcoming and hospitable presence to what is shared with us. This is an invitation to everyone engaged in this ministry to be self-reflective about the quality of presence being offered to another.

While expounding on discernment, Carter brilliantly describes the process that takes us from noticing the way I am to deciding the way I choose, inviting exploration of dreams, images, and desires. This description provides a method and schema for being with directees when they are engaging their own life questions. Readers will undoubtedly find this helpful in the practice of the process of discernment.

The value of Carter's message is not limited to those with a degree in theology or decades of experience in spiritual direction—his insights reflect universal experience and wisdom.

Within this book, you will find the ministry well understood, and will be invited to be patient with yourself and others as the next right steps in life are being considered.

Thirteenth century Sufi poet and theologian Rumi writes, "Let the beauty of what you love, be what you do." Within these pages, Carter shares what he loves, and the multitude of ways he practices his love, in a way that will encourage and inspire its readers.

Lucy Abbott Tucker
SDI co-founder and international spiritual direction supervision instructor
August 2024

PREFACE

"All religious talk....is talk about the ultimate and the sacred as it appears in ordinary experience."[1]

—Langdon Gilkey (3)

Each of us, in our own way, needs to discover the sacred in what moves and touches us, in the ordinary rather than the extraordinary. Spiritual direction can become a place where we begin to put things together and find meaning and purpose in life. God, rather than an object "out there," becomes a lived experience, known from within. Here we learn to stop worrying whether the Bible or the Creeds are true and focus on the real question: "Am I true?"

When we come to spiritual direction, we are looked at respectfully and listened to in such a way that enables us to discover that we matter and that our greatest gift is to be able to say "I am." Here we can be real and open—in touch with our fears and anxieties, as well as our hopes and dreams—and wake up to the blessed realization that it is here, in the present moment, in our poverty of "unknowing," that this is the right place, and indeed the place of grace. The aim of spiritual direction is to create an environment where a genuine encounter with the ultimate Other can take place.

The questions asked in spiritual direction are not closed, but open-ended, helping us to pay attention to our reality, and hear the invitation embedded in that experience. *"What's* going on?" leads to other critical questions such as *"How* are you living with what's going

---

1 Langdon Gilkey, quoted in Dermot A. Lane, *The Experience of God: An Invitation to do Theology*. New York: Paulist Press, 1981.

on?" "Are you living in such a way that *leads to life*, freedom and compassion, or otherwise?" "Can you *imagine* life differently?" "Can you get in touch with what you really *want* in life?" and "Can you *tell it how it is?*" Spiritual direction at its best, honours both our words and our silences, offering a presence that takes us seriously in this sacred space.

Through the practice of spiritual direction, we learn that faith is not so much believing in a lot of things, but a disposition of openness and readiness to hear and see the reality of our everyday life. It is about living our life in reference to something beyond ourselves. It is where we learn that love is God's meaning and our meaning as well, that we exist for love, and that we have an inherent capacity for self-transcendence. It is where we discover that love opens us up towards the possibility of hope.

We are awakened to the reality of who we really are, where we belong, where we have come from, and what we are being invited to become. While vocation in many ways has to do with what we are called to do, our fundamental and primary vocation has to do with who we are being called to be. This is the dynamic process of becoming the person God is calling into being. When a person sees a spiritual director, she is offered a place where she can learn to value her embodied life, and where she can discover that the incarnation says to her that there is only one reality, which is the source and substance of all creation, and astonishingly, that we are a part of that reality. Being fully human and fully alive is our vocation, and spiritual direction helps us to become more fully ourselves.

And so, this profound practice helps us realize that God is not a possession, but a reality offering us new life and gifting us into a new world of possibilities, a future that is constantly calling us and shaping us even more strongly than our past. Waiting patiently with another, in the face of a silent and hidden God, is the very heart of spiritual direction. From here we can begin to see beyond the narrow confines of our pre-occupations and worries and disillusionment, and even our sense of hopelessness—all indications of that "small self" we only think is who we really are—and live out of that deep centre of the human heart, our True Self, where God both speaks and dwells.

At the heart of spiritual direction is a journey towards discernment, where we learn to live as congruently and authentically as possible. Learning to be open to what *is*, we begin to understand that faith is a habit of the heart, a way of being in the world which leads to both life and freedom. Our disposition is crucial: it helps us to attend to the inner and often hidden movements within us which lead towards or away from life. Made in the image of God, we are image makers and image bearers, and it is through our imaginations, that we can discover attractive and alternative ways of being and living, and where we can tap into our deepest desires and find the courage to make life transforming choices.

What is offered in spiritual direction is a spacious place, where we find room to breathe and begin to experience what we already have and who we already are. It is the place of transformation, where we can bring our lived reality, with all its failings and flaws, as well as its creativity and possibility, into a larger context which gives it new meaning. This is the space God clears for us in Jesus, who makes it possible for us to live where he lives, where our very human reality and the goodness and love of God belong together, and where we discover the mystery and miracle of the new creation.

He showed me this little thing, the size of a hazelnut, on the palm of my hand, round like a ball. I looked at it thoughtfully and wondered, "What is this?" And the answer came, "It is all that is made". I marvelled that it continued to exist and did not suddenly disintegrate; it was so small. And again my mind supplied the answer, "It exists, both now and for ever, because God loves it.

—Julian of Norwich, Revelations of Divine Love

We came all this way to explore the moon, and the most important thing is that we discovered the Earth.

—Bill Anders, Apollo 8, 1968

My view of our planet (Earth) was a glimpse of divinity.

—Edgar Mitchell, Apollo 14, 1971

PART I

"A gifted presence to help a gifted self emerge"

—Shaun McCarty (104-5)

CHAPTER ONE

Listened into Speech: A Conversation That Can Make a Difference[2]

In his book *Conversation: How Talk Can Change Our Lives*, internationally acclaimed thinker and writer Theodore Zeldin asks, "How can conversations make so much difference?" His response is that "they can't if you believe that the world is ruled by overpowering economic and political forces, that conflict is the essence of life, that humans are basically animals, and that history is just a long struggle for survival and domination. If that's true, you can't change much. All you can do is have conversations which distract or amuse you. *But I see the world differently, as made of individuals searching for a partner, for a lover, for a guru, for God.* The most important, life-changing events are the meetings of these individuals" (Zeldin, 4).

There are many ways to talk about the spiritual dimension to life, and experiences of searching, belonging, meaning, depth, and transformation underlie them all. It is in this understanding of ourselves and our world that spiritual direction finds its place. At its most basic, spiritual direction is a conversation, where silence is as important as the words themselves. Spiritual direction is not concerned with certainties or creedal statements. Less about answers than questions, spiritual direction seeks to move away from judgments and achievements, constantly returning to who I am, and through that, ever turning towards new directions. It is about discovering the possibilities that are endlessly offered to us, simply through the creative dispositions

---

2 Chapter One: First published in *Eremos: Exploring Spirituality in Australia*. December, 2017. Reprinted by permission

we bring to life situations. In spiritual direction, we find a place for us to explore and listen, and to wake up and wonder at the energy, life, wisdom, and grace found at the heart of all things.

"A pressure of significance"

Australian poet Les Murray has spoken of moments that occurred in his life that were freighted with meaning and that spoke of another world. "From earliest childhood, I was always conscious of a strong, sometimes frightening, sometimes deeply necessary current of sheer meaning in things and people, *a pressure of significance* that only rarely carried over into what people commonly said. The world was resonant and radiant with meanings, and, knowing this, how could I speak as if none of it mattered, or leave it out the way people seemed to do" (Tacey, 112).

When a person first comes to spiritual direction, she is often not aware of just how "resonant and radiant with meanings" her world is. She finds herself somewhere in between excitement and apprehension. She wants something, though she may not be able to name what it is. She may be in pain or distress, though unsure of just how much she is hurting. She has taken a bold step in seeking someone to talk to. As she speaks, she begins to get in touch with the kind of "pressure" Les Murray alludes to that is seeking expression, release, or resolution. She may not even be aware of just how significant this pressure is, but this journey that she has begun will hopefully alert her over time, not only to its meaning, but also to its challenge and its invitation.

For such a conversation, she instinctively knows that she needs a safe and encouraging place to share her story. She will also need patience, courage, and persistence. Just as one can hear, for example, the Beatitude about the poor in spirit only through one's own lack or poverty, so too in this emotional and spiritual transaction that is spiritual direction can she only find a certain freedom through encountering and expressing her truth. She may not see herself as a person of faith.

She may well shy away from such terms as *discipleship*, but in her willingness for relationship—and the intimacy, honesty, and vulnerability that that implies—she is learning, by going where she needs to go.

"You and me both"

One of the consequences of thinking about who Jesus was and what he taught, has been to ignore *how* he was in relation to others. The preference for a propositional, rather than dispositional theology has led us to downplay his transformational way of being with others.

In his book *Death Sentence: The Decay of Public Language*, Australian writer Don Watson says that when a speaker addresses an audience, he is "attempting an embrace, he is saying to his listeners, *'you and me both'*" (Watson, 139). This phrase captures something of the self-emptying that is at the heart of Jesus, the one who makes space for the other. The Gospels are full of stories where Jesus meets individuals and he elicits from them their deepest needs or desires; as a result, they find within themselves the possibility of taking the next step towards life and healing. It is as if Jesus "believes" people into letting go of their life-denying attitudes and behaviors so that they can become all they can be.

The persuasive character of the Incarnation is that God becomes as one of us (like us in every respect, though without sin) so that we may wake up to the fact that we are like him. Here, in the person and manner of Jesus of Nazareth, is a wonderful way of being for the spiritual director. When someone realizes that the person she is opening up to—beginning to share her deepest self with—is actually embodying the words *you and me both*, she instinctively knows she is both accepted and understood, not in the sense that she is now "defined" or "explained" but rather encountered, in solidarity, by a fellow human being.

Our deepest need is to be recognized

One of the most telling remarks of Jesus in the Gospels is when he is in the house of Simon the Pharisee. When a woman bathes Jesus's feet with her tears and wipes them with her hair, Simon mutters to himself that if Jesus were a prophet he would have known what kind of woman this was. Jesus says to Simon: "Do you see this woman?" Of course he had seen her at one level. But he had already judged her, and in consequence, missed her completely.

Australian social commentator Hugh Mackay says that "all of us yearn to be taken seriously." He suggests that "being truly, seriously listened to feels like a welcome and precious gift" and means that ultimately another person's welfare, hopes, and fears matter as much as one's own. To be seen by another, heard, and listened to in both speech and life—which is the very heart of spiritual direction—conveys the priceless miracle that "I matter" (Mackay, 29).

"One gesture will do it"

Francis of Assisi, on one famous occasion, overcame his fear and revulsion to embrace a leper. This singular moment speaks powerfully of the truth that "you cannot love an abstraction" (Huddleston, 247). G. K. Chesterton knew that the great gift Francis brought to his every encounter with others was no mere "abstract enthusiasm," nor "mere pity." He says that Francis "only saw the image of God multiplied but never monotonous...." Chesterton clearly explains, "No plans or proposals or efficient rearrangements will give back to a broken man his self-respect and sense of speaking with an equal. *One gesture will do it*" (Chesterton, 110-11).

Words are obviously part of what makes the spiritual direction session. Words spoken with care, with a sense of their power and capacity to carry meaning, invite a person to listen even more deeply and intently and to enter the space where T. S Eliot remarks, "Words, after speech, reach/Into the silence" (Eliot, 19). Silence is important because, as Alastair Campbell reminds us, words can seduce and conceal what the simplicity and "richness of silence" can alone reveal (Campbell, 60–61).

Clearly, words and images are only part of what is going on in any conversation. We are embodied beings. Our bodies convey so much—the way we sit, the way we look, our centeredness and stillness, and our sense of belonging in this place and at this time. All "speak" into the depths of another's being. So, we must never underestimate the power of a single gesture. As we sit with others, we learn to trust that this work, initiated by the grace of God, where someone seeks me out to talk to, may bear much fruit in people's lives. I don't manipulate anything here. I do not engineer any particular outcome. I simply entrust myself to another, and in the simplicity and poverty of my lived experience, I surrender this encounter to God.

"The more there is that happens"

The great U.S. twentieth-century psychotherapist Carl Rogers wrote how "hearing has consequences. When I truly hear a person and the meanings that are important to him at that moment, hearing not simply his words, but him, and when I let him know that I have heard his own private personal meanings, many things happen. There is first of all a grateful look. He feels released. He wants to tell me more about his world. He surges forth in a new sense of freedom. He becomes more open to the process of change. I have often noticed that the more deeply I hear the meanings of this person, *the more there is that happens*" (Rogers, 10).

Where there is genuine mutuality, something happens. There is a shift or reorientation. Not seeing different things but seeing things differently. This is a deep, intuitive realization that things cannot be the same again, an imaginative jolt that can give me the courage to do the one thing needful. It is an experience of regaining contact with something I had lost or repudiated, aspects of myself that I could never have imagined were full of grace. Saying "here I am" offers the possibility of coming home to myself, to the "inner room" Jesus talks about. We often realize that the things that have so impeded us and held us back are not the truest thing about us, but rather invitations into a deeper and richer awareness of who we really are. Here, as the disciples discovered, in their upper room after the shock of the crucifixion and resurrection, walls can become a window where we catch a glimpse of an undreamt future calling us.

"A small, shy truth arrives"

Yet whatever breakthrough occurs, it is not the end of the story. Life is still to be lived. Choices are still to be made. Anxieties and fears will still be present. We still need to come down from the mountain. But, as Australian cartoonist Michael Leunig says, "A small, shy truth arrives" (Leunig). It is "small" because it is often hesitant, a hint of a possible future, a seeing that is both indistinct and imperfect. It is "shy" and hidden, concealing as much as revealing. It is "truth," but not so much a conceptual grasp of an objective reality as it is a discovery of oneself so that I can begin to say, "I am." Here, in a wonderful phrase by novelist Marilynne Robinson, "Consciousness has the character of revelation"—a revelation, a truth that just "arrives," from without and within (Robinson, xiv).

This moment is truly an event of grace, a moment of the Spirit. Like the disciples of Jesus in Mark's Gospel, however, we often do not get it at first, and for most of us, it usually takes a long time to work things out. Our biggest problem, according to Rowan Williams (42), is that when confronted with the truth, we do not know that we don't know. Which is why the conversation that happens in spiritual direction is important. St. Augustine knew about this moment; he knew that this is the place to stay. It is why he could say, "We have not yet found what we are seeking, but we have found where to look for it" (Taylor,

Christlike God, 24). The unusual "healing by stages" of the blind man in Mark 8:22–26 could be helpful here. Before his sight is fully restored, he says, "I can see people, but they look like trees walking." Perhaps growth in faith is more often a slow process of "putting things together" than an assured sense of having figured it all out.

The discovery, best described as a revelation, happens not all at once but rather little by little. Utterly true to our experience, it is often a case of one step forward and two steps back! It is not surprising then that Mark's Gospel, where discipleship is so central, ends, in its original form, abruptly, with the women fleeing the tomb in terror and amazement. The point is surely not lost on us, that here we are being invited into our own lived experience, to put things together, and to take the next step into the participatory knowing of surrender, moving beyond where we are to a new place and a new attitude. It is now that we learn how "conversation" is linked etymologically to "conversion." In the conversation, which is spiritual direction, I am not invited to run away from who I am but rather to stay there—or perhaps I should say *here*—and discover in the intimacy and vulnerability of this place my ever-present need to change and grow and be transformed.

CHAPTER TWO

An "exchange of gifts"

We are relational beings. We find ourselves only through each other. "Created as hearer of the Word" and "conceived in the mind of God as the partner in a dialogue" (Balthasar, 18–9), we are caught up in what Pope Paul VI called a "dialogue of salvation" (Paul VI, Section 38). Pope John Paul II developed this and saw that "[this] capacity for 'dialogue' is rooted in the nature of the person and his dignity." This ongoing conversation that God has with the world, if it is to be true and creative, will always be an "exchange of gifts" and not simply an exchange of ideas (John Paul II, Section 28). Such conversation will be an act of love, a place for engagement and encounter, and a revelatory event, where truth comes forth.

Creating a Culture of Conversation

A word is dead, when it is said
Some say—
I say it just begins to live
That day.

—Dickinson (*Poem* 278)

Genuine dialogue will always seek to be mutual because it implies an embrace of the other, something shared, a recognition that we are in this together. A potent image for such dialogue is "open arms" (Volf, 141-144). In the Gospels, Jesus is always turning us away from ourselves towards the other, the stranger, the one different from us, and even the enemy, all of whom offer us the face of God. Noticing, listening, and attending to the other in spiritual direction will always mean shifting from my concerns and preoccupations, leaving my world, and entering into the other's world. Entering, and for a time inhabiting, the other's world is demanding, and invites me into nothing less than conversion. Such a conversion asks me to see the other not as someone who will hinder my becoming fully alive, fully human, but someone who draws me into the fullness and dignity of being able to say to them, "Here I am." The skills I have learned, and which are crucial in so many ways, I can set aside, or even forget, trusting, in that precious moment, the giftedness of simply being present.

And being present in such a way, I can move from being self-centered and self-absorbed and, with the eyes of my heart opened, begin to see how the other can gift me. French poet Charles Péguy held to a vision that "We must all be saved together, we all need to reach Paradise together; we must all arrive in Heaven together. We must think of others, we must give ourselves to others. What will God say to us if we appear in Heaven without the others?" (Mendonça, 41). In modern times, no one speaks more clearly than former South African bishop Desmond Tutu about how "We need other human beings in order to be human. I am because other people are.... A person is a person through other persons" (Tutu, 3).

Considering all this, we can begin to see how significant spiritual direction could be in the creation of a culture of conversation, marked by availability, welcome, receptivity, respect, care, and compassion, albeit in a hidden and unassuming way. As spiritual directors, we are to take seriously the words we speak and the words we hear spoken. They can be quite literally sacraments of mystery, depth, and also, surprise. One of the marvelous things about spiritual direction—if we can notice and let go of our tendency to preempt or categorize those who come to see us—is the sheer fact that both of us can be surprised, and inspired, by the totally unexpected.

In the lovely poem by Emily Dickinson that prefaces this section, the "aliveness" of the spoken word is celebrated. That living word, spoken and received in a spirit of integrity and truthfulness, like the Word of God, is more of a happening, an event, rather than a thing, dispositional rather than propositional, opening us to a lived encounter with God. Some of these words we share in the spiritual direction relationship will be what Roman Catholic twentieth-century theologian Karl Rahner, SJ, called "primordial words," which he said are like "sea-shells, in which can be heard the sound of the ocean of infinity, no matter how small they are in themselves" (Rahner, 295-296).

This suggests that there is much more to communication than the simple sharing of facts or ideas, for the "deepest level of communication is not communication, but communion" (Merton, *Asian Journal*, 308). When we genuinely engage in dialogue, we are not trying to manipulate or persuade. Our dialogue suggests that we are in a common search for a truth that we do not or cannot contain, a truth that draws us on and deeper. We are about creating an environment that makes communion possible. As spiritual directors, we are to create such conditions where encounter with mystery becomes possible, and where our meeting together opens us both to an "event of communion," an "event of the Spirit" (Edwards, 28, 173). The word "event" comes from the Latin "e" and "venire" meaning "to come out," so such an event as the spiritual direction encounter is a moment or opportunity for the Divine or the Real to come out or shine forth (Whelan, 126).

...still and still moving
Into another intensity
For a further union, a deeper communion

—Eliot (32)

"Don" had been seeing me for some time. He was a Catholic religious brother, and had been so for around forty years, a vocation that had blessed him and which he had engaged in fully and with great faithfulness. On this

particular day he arrived and said that he was a little embarrassed because he had nothing to report on his devotional life. I indicated that this was no problem for me and that I was happy for him simply to tell me what was going on for him. He began to talk, and for the next thirty minutes or so held me spellbound with his story. His dilemma, a word that scarcely captures what was happening for him, was that he had fallen in love. When he finally stopped talking, and after considerable silence, I (somewhat provocatively) said, "Well, you wouldn't want to spoil that by having a devotional life!" He smiled, for I think he knew in that instant that I had heard him, really heard him, and indeed honoured him. And I knew, as he was speaking, that we were on holy ground. I had nothing but admiration and a deep respect for his courage and integrity in the way he was grappling with what faced him. What he was only just beginning to see then, of course, and what he continued over the coming months to explore with me, was the clash between two seemingly irreconcilable vocations. I was later privileged to read a lesson at the service where he formally took leave of his (gracious) community, and to be present at his subsequent wedding. Truly an "exchange of gifts!"

Making Space

To be fully alive and fully human, we need space, or room to breathe. This need is fundamental, and it is rooted in our everyday experience. We all know what it is like to feel crowded, pressed, or overwhelmed. We know what it is like to face deadlines, expectations, demands. We know these pressures can originate from outside us as well as from within us. And we know the relief, release, and freedom that come from outer and inner space—room to breathe and to be ourselves. We owe it to ourselves, individually and communally, to find such room, such space.

This is the space that we might say God clears for us, in which we can find our inherent worth and value. When we read the Gospels, we see Jesus of Nazareth as one who continually creates a space, one who is unreservedly receptive—and he does this because he has cleared a space within himself for the other, a place where genuine encounter and engagement could take place. This is a space and place that is participatory, freeing, inclusive, accepting, and transformative. This is certainly the basis of his attractiveness and authority. Of Jesus we could say that he created the conditions such that the poor, those on the edge and the marginalized, those who were sick and outcast, could believe enough in themselves that they were able to call out to him expectantly. Such is the fruit of offering space to others.

Years ago, "Frank," a university lecturer, came to see me in a very distressed state. His wife had left him. His world had been shattered. He felt defeated and ashamed. His position in a large evangelical church as a Bible study leader was, for him, untenable. When I asked him what he really wanted, he replied, "I want my wife back." I continued to see him, keen to be supportive and keen to see, in this story of failure and despair, any sign of God's grace at work. Over the next few sessions with him, I would gently return to the question, "But what do you really want in all this?" And he kept answering, in a sad and bewildered way, "I want my wife back." It was all he could see. Imagine my delight, when one day, in answer to my constant question, he replied, "I want to live properly." He paused, smiled weakly, and said, "I also want my wife back." With that smile, he indicated that he somehow knew—and wanted me to know—that he had turned a corner, that at last he was in touch with a deeper, Godly desire, that his was the beginning, as indeed it was, of a long, painful recovery towards living properly. Instead of staying stuck, endlessly caught in reducing his life simply to what had happened to him, somehow "Frank" found some space, some room to move, to begin to believe and honour his sense of self, his "I am."

So, when we talk about God, one of the attractive things we can say is that in the infinity of God there is room for the finite, for otherness; that God "makes room" for creation by constricting divine power. The eminent theologian Jürgen Moltmann says that the Trinitarian community of God is "so wide that the whole creation can find space, time and freedom in it." The creation of the universe, he suggests, involves a "withdrawal" of God in order to make space for creation

(Moltmann,109-110).

When Saint Paul came to think deeply on the person of Jesus, he came to see that he reflected precisely this same self-emptying, for he "did not regard equality with God as something to be exploited, but emptied himself" making room, giving space (Phil 2: 6–7). The feminist theologian Elizabeth Johnson says, "To be so structured that you have room inside yourself for another is quintessentially a female experience" (Johnson, 234). Making room for another, which is of course what we do in spiritual direction, is then always going to be fundamentally about birthing, creativity, and new life.

Fostering Silence

In the spiritual direction relationship, as directees, we need a safe and encouraging space, where we can speak openly about what concerns us—about our hopes and fears, our sorrows and joys. As trust grows, we can begin to express ourselves more deeply and fully, but we need not be surprised that our language gives way to silence, as we let go of the struggle to find the appropriate words and learn, through the patience of the spiritual director, how to begin to savour our experience. Integral to any language, of course, is silence, and the intervals between the words are as important as the words themselves.

Silence makes possible a true conversation with ourselves, with others, and with God. Far from being an absence of words, it offers both possibility and opportunity. According to the philosopher and writer Ivan Illich, there is a silence of availability or "deep interest" (the very heart of spiritual direction), a silence of nourishment and growth (where the reign of God can grow imperceptibly, like a mustard seed), the silence beyond words (where we are addressed by God), and the silence of the Pieta (where in the silence of suffering we face the mystery of death and discover the power of compassion in our poverty) (Illich, 42-46).

Whose silence so eloquent as his?
What word so explosive
as that one Palestinian
word with the endlessness of its fallout?

—Thomas (317)

The silence, that "severer listening," (Rich, 75) that we are called to as spiritual directors, involves a radical stripping away, a release from any fantasy that we might have about ourselves and any illusion that we might be under about our abilities to help, constantly distancing ourselves from those hidden needs for admiration, control, or influence that distort and block us from the freeing and creative influence of grace. We are indeed "value-bearers who are good for the other," but we are also "value-concealers whose own needs and distortions of reality may have a negative effect on the free unfolding" of those who come to see us (Gratton, *Guidelines for Spiritual Direction*, 185). Silence alone can bear the full weight of what we are attempting to say about God's relationship with the world and with us. Silence alone can help us face the deepest and darkest truths of life and help us refuse to accept any palliative that holds us back from the reality of the living God.

As a spiritual director, I am sure that I am not alone when I say there have been many times in offering direction that I have not known what to say. While in the past this may have been either an opportunity to say something anyway, or to bewail my inadequacy in the role, I have come to see that by simply noticing this, and letting it go, I am able to get in touch with and live out of a deeper sense of who I am, that I can be fully present and delight in this moment as a moment of grace and opportunity.

Hesitation, Understanding, and Waiting

The dispositions we bring to spiritual direction are crucial, and the

Zen Buddhist concept of "beginner's mind," in which "there are many possibilities, but in the expert's, there are few," offers a helpful frame (Suzuki, 21). As we listen to someone or study scriptures, we need to strive toward a beginner's mind—a disposition of newness, free of certainty, and even a willingness to be wrong, so that words may be truly heard. Because we are not an assured, self-contained accomplishment, we can begin to see that our human becoming rests in our capacity to be available and receptive.

Hesitation is not a disposition we immediately connect with spiritual direction. To hesitate is not always seen as a virtue. We even say that the one who hesitates is lost, implying that there is something lacking. Theologian and former archbishop of Canterbury Rowan Williams suggests, following French philosopher Simone Weil, that hesitation is what "we ought to feel in the presence ... of a human other. Whenever we meet someone else ... we hesitate, we don't assume we understand them, (or that) we have enclosed them ... captured them" (Williams, 81)

In our encounter with another, we draw back, in humility and expectancy. Reflecting on his experience of being in New York at the time of the events of terrorist attack on September 11, 2001, Rowan Williams wrote *Writing in the Dust*. At the end of the book, he mentions the time in the gospels when Jesus encounters the woman caught in adultery (Jn 8:1–11), where he bends down and, enigmatically, writes in the dust. Rather than rush in, Jesus pauses, hesitates, allowing "a longish moment, in which people are given time to see themselves differently precisely because he refuses to make the sense they want." This is "writing in the dust," Williams concludes, because it tries to hold that moment for "a little longer, long enough for some of our demons to walk away" (Williams, 81).

So even when we say we understand someone or something, we need to be careful. If we can think of understanding in terms of standing under, "suggestive of a certain posture," we can be released from trying to grasp or even comprehend, which can so easily mean mastery or control. Standing under allows us to become like an understanding friend who is wanting to be attentive, open to receive, respectful, and patient (Vanstone, *Fare Well*, 27).

Sometimes in a spiritual direction session, when I feel the inner urge to say something, I catch myself asking whether these words are for myself or for the other. Such a question stops me in my tracks and offers me another way of seeing, another way of being, a kind of wisdom that allows me to wait, and to discern the kairos time of opportunity and possibility.

Waiting is at the very heart of spiritual direction, but of course, it is not easy. We get impatient in a world of fast food, instant coffee, and mass information at our fingertips on the internet. We want things, and we want them now. Waiting proves to be both intense and poignant. It has a way with us, stripping us of illusion and self-deception. We do not, and cannot, possess God, we must wait for God. Perhaps waiting is the one thing we can do with some kind of assurance. Simone Weil says, "We do not obtain the most precious gifts by going in search of them but by waiting for them.... The soul empties itself of all its own contents in order to receive the human being it is looking at, just as he is, in all his truth" (Weil, 73, 75). Waiting imbues what we wait for with meaning and value, and as we wait, we are somehow grasped by that for which we wait. We wait beyond words and explanations for a deeper truth to reveal itself, for with God there is always more.

Many years ago, in a spiritual direction session, a woman was describing the very dark place she was in, and the despair that was threatening to overwhelm her. As I listened, I became painfully aware of my inability to say or do anything that might help, that anything I might say would be an intrusion. I could only wait. In that waiting, I realized I could only continue this ministry as a person of hope. I was struck by the fact that if I was not a person of hope, I would have to stop offering spiritual direction. I did not reason this out, nor was it something contrived, it was simply given. Somehow hope had captured me, offering me a way of being in the world and with others that made sense, despite all the appearances to the contrary. It was not as if I knew how things would turn out. I was not blind to the realities of the situation, nor was I unaware of the challenges and choices that would have to be faced. But what a difference it makes to be with someone and listen from a place of hope. It was only through the poverty of waiting that I woke up, that I didn't have to have all the answers, or even words, for I knew then, as I still do, is that because of my poverty, what I could do was to be with others and for others, as a person of hope.

When I speak
Though it be you who speak
Through me, something is lost.
The meaning is in the waiting.

—Thomas (199)

It is here that genuine hope is born, for hope is not "optimism in the conventional sense, by which we usually mean the belief that 'everything will turn out well'". This is why Vaclav Havel could say that faith is crucial, the faith that is the "ability to see things as they really are, for everything—even what turns out badly—has its own admittedly obscure meaning in relation to faith" (Havel, 150, 153). In waiting, we experience that somehow the world matters, that it is important, reflecting how God is with the creation. Having expended all in creative endeavour, God waits. Waiting "enacts and discloses that which, at the deepest level, is distinctive of divinity, distinctive of God" (Vanstone, *Stature*, 89). Surely the most poignant image of such waiting—disclosing the power of waiting—is the way Jesus is portrayed in the Gospels, handing himself over, moving from action to passion, and in so doing, revealing the depths of self-giving love. This is love's risk.

"Grace is ... everywhere"
—Bernanos (317)

The spiritual direction relationship is both beautiful and gracious, and we must never lose the sense of awe and privilege when we are in the presence of another person. We scarcely need promote ourselves, for there is something inherently attractive and attracting about this ministry. There is about it, in French philosopher Paul Ricœur's words, an experience of the "dynamics of delight" (Gratton, *Art of Spiritual Guidance*, 132). It is like a person stumbling on a treasure in a field who sells all that he has in order to buy the field. Selling all only makes sense in light of finding the treasure. As spiritual directors, we need to remind ourselves constantly of this treasure.

But as Saint Paul says, it is a "treasure we have in clay jars" (2 Cor 4:7). We need to have enough sight to know we are blind, enough life to know we are dying, that we are limited fragile creatures, and often conflicted. With Thomas Merton, we can recognize that our inconsistencies are nothing but the revelation of who we are. "I am thrown into contradiction: to realize it is mercy, to accept it is love, and to help others do the same is compassion" (Merton, Learning to Love, 355). But the miracle of grace is this: "I must give to others not only something that is my own but my very self; I must be personally present in my gift" (Benedict XVI, 34).

The Greek root word *charis*, gives context to the amazing thing about grace, the reciprocal nature of gift and gratitude. As we come for spiritual direction, and as we offer it, we are caught up in this giving and receiving. It is certainly something attractive and attracting. It is at best, always gracious and generous. It is surprisingly, as an "event of the Spirit," both gift and response, indeed, an "exchange of gifts." No wonder it has been said, "'A gifted presence to help a gifted self emerge'—that is how I see spiritual direction" (McCarty, 104–05).

CHAPTER THREE

"Attention is our daily bread"[3]

The spiritual director who prepares for and arrives at the spiritual direction session with the dispositions of welcome and hospitality, availability and receptivity, reminds herself of the overwhelming importance of the gift of being present. She has "nothing to offer unless she offers to be present, really and totally present, really and totally *in* the present" (John Taylor, *Primal Vision*, 189). In this face-to-face encounter of true presence, her questions must be respectful, honouring the differences between herself and the other. The director is not turning the direction session into an interrogation, nor is she intrusive or controlling. Far from diminishing him, her inquiries should give him increase through the non-manipulative simplicity of asking open-ended questions. Closed questions result in "Yes" or "No" answers, whereas open questions invite further exploration. As the poet Rilke famously wrote, "try to live *the questions themselves,*"and "*live* [them] for now. Perhaps then you will gradually, without noticing it, live your way into an answer, one distant day in the future" (Rilke, 17).

Behind each question lie some fundamental convictions. John V. Taylor felt the issue revolved around whether our disposition or attitude was either life-giving or life-denying: "It has long been my conviction that God is not hugely concerned as to whether we are religious or not. What matters to God, and matters supremely, is whether we are alive or not. If your religion brings you more fully to life, God

---

3   This title of this chapter comes from Iris Murdoch's *The Sovereignty of Good*, London: Routledge & Kegan Paul, 1971, 42.

will be in it; but if your religion inhibits your capacity for life or makes you run away from it, you may be sure God is against it, just as Jesus was" (Taylor, *Matter of Life and Death*, 18).

The enigmatic Roman Catholic intellectual Simone Weil's conviction was that telling the truth, *my* truth—at whatever personal cost—was paramount: "Christ likes us to prefer truth to him because, before being Christ, he is truth. If one turns aside from him to go towards the truth, one will not go far before falling into his arms" (Weil, 36).

For philosopher John McMurray, it was fear that holds us back from the truth that sets us free, echoing Jesus' message, "Do not be afraid": "The maxim of illusory religion runs: 'Fear not; trust in God and he will see that none of the things you fear will happen to you'. That of real religion, on the contrary, is 'Fear not; the things you are afraid of are quite likely to happen to you, but they are nothing to be afraid of'" (Barry, 126).

C. S. Lewis' fundamental conviction was that our desire, or lack of desire, puts us in touch with what God desires for us: "...it would seem that Our Lord finds our desires, not too strong, but too weak. We are half-hearted creatures, fooling about with drink and sex and ambition when infinite joy is offered us" (Lewis, 22).

The questions asked by the spiritual director are always in the service of the directee, helping to identify and clarify what he might bring. Sometimes a question can be put to slow down the pace, giving the directee time to reflect and savour what he is experiencing. The questions themselves are not so much for communication, however important that is, but, in their very simplicity, are gateways towards an insight, and even more importantly, an encounter, where the directee experiences being addressed and eventually, a deepening awareness of the presence of mystery, in whom our being dwells and moves.

The questions presuppose a climate of silence and patience, where God, utterly transcendent and immanent, "over" and "in" all things, as the writer of the letter to the Ephesians says, becomes transparent, "through" all things. The preparation for spiritual direction, as well as the session itself, and the reflection afterwards, are all in the service of this sacramental understanding of the relationship between God and the world. Expressing our experiences of joy and sadness, fear and hope, our belief and doubt are sacramental expressions of who we really are. Being made in the image of God we are image bearers and image makers. As Theseus says in Shakespeare's *A Midsummer Night's Dream*, "imagination bodies forth the form of things/Unknown" (Act V, Scene I). In this way the spiritual director helps us realize that we cannot apprehend these very human experiences until they find expression. The very real experiences of our lives, so often too deep or too painful for us to face, are here called out from us and given shape and form. Being given the opportunity to express ourselves, to give voice to our truth, we realize that this moment carries with it the possibility of revelation and transformation.

What?

... so in everyday life
it is the plain facts and natural happenings
that conceal God and reveal him to us
little by little under the mind's tooling.

—R. S. Thomas (355)

Spiritual direction is reality based. It is about "living the given life, and not the planned" (Berry, III, 150). It is not about aiding or encouraging a piety that escapes from or denies what is. It knows that relationships with self, with God, and with others thrive on reality and honesty.

Such attention to reality was expressed by Simone Weil in *Waiting on God* with great simplicity and directness: "The love of our neighbor in all its fullness simply means being able to say to him, 'What are you going through?'" (Weil, 75). And Weil knew that paying attention was not an end in itself, but that it carried with it its own inner potential for transformation writing, "Never ... is a genuine effort of the attention wasted.... The attention is creative" (Weil, 67, 103). The spiritual director encourages the spiritual directee in the art of paying attention, both through example and by her manner of questioning.

On the road to Emmaus, the two disciples were both bewildered and disappointed. Their hopes had been dashed, and the stranger who was with them asked them about the things they were discussing with each other while they were walking along. "What things?" he said (Lk 24:17, 19). Little by little, Jesus invited them into their own story, to notice and identify their present experience. And in the telling of their story, deeper insights came to the surface.

When the spiritual director asks, "What things?" she is, "listening the spiritual directee into speech," helping him to hear, perhaps for the first time, hidden fears and anxieties, hopes and dreams. In this way, she is gently and patiently preparing the way for him to begin to look at his story in a different light, a bigger context. What is going on? What are you living with? What are you carrying? And what is that like for you?

How?

The question before me, now that I
am old is not how to be dead,
which I know from enough practice,
but how to be alive

—(Berry VI, 222)

We need to be in touch with the fundamental realities of our lives, for here we find the human starting points for religious faith, according to Michael Paul Gallagher (93-94). But our attitude, the way we respond to the circumstances of our lives, is crucial. Lecturer and writer Ronald Rolheiser, OMI's reminder about "the fire that burns within," what some people call "pre-religious God awareness," has tremendous implications for those of us who are responding to the call into spiritual direction and who find ourselves walking with people of a particular faith tradition, or no faith tradition at all.

"Long before we do anything explicitly religious at all, we have to do something about the fire that burns within us. What we do with that fire, how we channel it, is our spirituality.... And how we do channel it, the disciplines and habits we choose to live by, will either lead to a greater integration or disintegration within our bodies, minds and souls, and to a greater integration or disintegration in the way we are related to God, others, and the cosmic world" (Rolheiser, 6, 11).

St John of the Cross saw clearly that "what matters is not what happens but how one responds to what happens" (Gallagher, *Dive Deeper*, 93). Michael Paul Gallagher speaks of how the Bible "communicates on a non-doctrinal level- that of story, of experience, of slow discovery." He suggests that "our crucial hungers are more human than explicitly religious" so the focus for the spiritual direction conversation will be a person's "pre-religious God awareness" (Moore, 35). The invitation here is to "evoke human experiences of depth and to ponder them as the theatre of the Spirit" (Gallagher, *Dive Deeper,* 3).

This has tremendous implications for those of us who are responding to the call into spiritual direction and who find ourselves walking with people of a particular faith tradition, or no faith tradition at all. The exchange between the spiritual director and directee will necessarily be, at least initially, "on the human level, marked by honesty and depth, about what people really live, and about what they have experienced in privileged moments of their past" (Gallagher, *Free to Believe*, 15). A person's lived experience—their relationships, experience of failure, awareness of the world's pain, experience of solitude and the reality of their quite ordinary lives—all this becomes the very focus of the spiritual direction exchange and the starting points for faith. For faith, far from being belief in a doctrinal statement, is a "God-given way of imagining existence" (Gallagher, Dive Deeper, 6), a waking up to the mystery and depth at the heart of all things. Faith always refers to something beyond ourselves, and is fundamentally an openness of heart. It this disposition and attitude towards life which carries with it the promise of discovering the extraordinary in the everyday and opens a person up to exploring the sources of wonder that too often are ignored or neglected.

So, the questions we find ourselves asking revolve around one of the most important words in the spiritual life: How? How are you living with your "what"? Are you living with your circumstances, temperament, others, in such a way that helps you to greater integration or disintegration? Does your attitude lead you towards or away from life? Towards or away from freedom, compassion, and hope?

What If?

One day people will touch and talk perhaps easily,
And loving be natural as breathing and warm as sunlight...

—A. S. J. Tessimond (48)

What moves us is not reason or logic, but the imagination, as theologian and philosopher John Henry Newman saw. The imagination is our God-given way of handling reality. Jesus himself appealed not to our reason so much as to our hearts, our imaginations, and the centerpiece of his teaching, and great gift to us, was the Kingdom or Reign of God. This attractive, imaginative, and alternative vision of reality is offered to us in our everyday lives. It is not something we work for, but something we discover or wake up to—like someone stumbling on a treasure buried in a field.

The imagination, speaking the language of transcendence, opens us to the deepest levels of truth. Through the imagination, spiritual director and teacher Kathleen Fischer notes that we "experience ...

the Ultimate coming through finite reality," and in this sense we can say that the imagination "bridges the gap between matter and spirit" (Fischer, 8). The imaginative and symbolic life is evocative rather than explanatory and disposes us towards both possibility and promise. In this sense, according to Anselm Grün, "Images are forms of transport. They get us going. They move us on" (Grün, 4). As a source of knowledge, the imagination is always participatory, revelatory, and transformative. The question we are asking here is simply, What if? Can you imagine things differently? And what if you looked at life differently?

What Do You Want?

Tell me, what is it you plan to do
with your one wild and precious life?

—Mary Oliver (54)

But looking at things differently, however illuminating, is not enough. The faith that wakes up to the reality of God's presence and the offer of the Reign of God carries within it its own inner dynamic. It is true, "I learn by going where I have to go," according to Theodore Roethke (Roethke, 30). There is a performative aspect about faith: We venture or risk the next step, and we make choices. It is not a "leap in the dark" so much as the cumulative, long, and patient process of question and doubt, pain and darkness, that brings us to a place of deeper "knowing," all the while admitting to the reality of "unknowing."

This way forward confronts us with the invitation to look at what we really want. What opens up for us is both the intimacy of our inner life and a sense of ultimacy, a kind of expansive horizon in which we begin to see what is really on offer. Prayer then becomes what Ann and Barry Ulanov call "the place where we sort out our desires, and where we are ourselves sorted out by the desires we choose to follow" (Ulanov, 20).

In the lovely story of the blind beggar Bartimaeus, which makes him an admirable companion for us, Jesus stands still. And amid all the inner and outer voices, Jesus, as spiritual director, calls out from Bartimaeus his deepest desire: "What do you want me to do for you?" (see Mk 10:46–52). Here Bartimaeus is being asked to "lose his life," that smaller, surface life that is so preoccupied with goals, fears, and desires, but a life that is not even remotely the whole of who he really is. This life, a life in which Bartimaeus longs for fulfillment but never finds it, must be surrendered. Bartimaeus throws off his cloak, and letting go of all those competing voices, finds his deepest voice.

We stay still, looking at our spiritual directee, letting all the inner and outer voices come to the surface; and through our presence and gentle encouragement, we offer the space for her to see and hear more clearly, finding the courage to find her voice. Simone Weil, building on her focus on attention, saw that "attention animated by desire is the whole foundation of religious practices" (Weil, 129). The spiritual director asks: But what is it that you really want? Can you get in touch with your deepest desire? As you look at what it is you want, can you see where this desire leads? Have you a sense that it leads to life and freedom and hope, or does it lead to further frustration, anxiety, or fear?

Can You Tell It How It Is?

She must learn again to speak
starting with I
starting with We
starting as the infant does
with her own true hunger
and pleasure

and rage

—Marge Piercy (97)

And all our questions, uttered with sensitivity, reticence, and respect, converge in our being there for the sake of others, and being with them in such a way that they feel emboldened to speak, to say how it is for them. What we offer, as spiritual directors, is nothing less than the spaciousness of God, a place which "has been cleared where the act of God and human reality are allowed to belong together without rivalry or fear. "The place where Jesus is," is "...where a confused humanity [can be] heard in all its variety, emotional turmoil and spiritual uncertainty" (Williams, *The Tablet*, 18-9).

When we ask if they have spoken to God about all this, and they respond, "But God already knows," we will explore with them how relationships thrive on reality, honesty, and intimacy. Of course God knows, but the reason for disclosing to God what is on our minds and hearts is not so much the content but the act of disclosing itself. Whatever it is we disclose becomes a way of "stand[ing] unprotected before God," says art historian Sister Wendy Beckett (Beckett, viii). This is a place of much vulnerability, a kind of "loving wounding," says novelist Robert Dessaix, where we are "softly penetrated to every corner by another's knowing gaze" (Dessaix, 254).

The questions we ask here will always be encouraging. We do not push. But can you tell me a bit more about this? Can you say how you are feeling when you tell me this? And as you tell me this, have you any sense of how God might be thinking or feeling, as God looks at you, and listens to you? There is a time, God's time, for everything, and we respect the other in this.

***

Spiritual direction offers both the spiritual directee and the spiritual director a chance to be authentic and real, without illusion or pretense. Here attention is paid, not on ourselves as private, autonomous, self-contained individuals, but as persons in relationship. Our circumstances, temperament, and gifts; the choices we make; the context of the world in which we find ourselves; and the stories and traditions we have inherited and chosen all contribute to the raw material for spiritual direction. The five questions suggested here offer us a way of getting in touch with this raw material, so that we can discover that there is always something else going on at the same time. We "gather all the fragments" (John 6:12) of our lives, and we pay attention, in the hope that we will wake up and respond to this "something else:" the movement, activity, and invitation of God.

CHAPTER FOUR

A Sacred Relationship Where Together We Can Grow in Faith, Love, and Hope[4]

The mystery of poetry lies in its capacity to speak a truth through words, silence, and space, and as contemporary poet Peter Jay has said, "We look to poetry for the thisness it encapsulates, and the otherness it evokes" (O'Driscoll, 132). Which precisely captures the genius of spiritual direction, for like poetry, spiritual direction encourages people to pay attention to the "thisness" or "givenness" of their life and at the same time to be open to the possibility of life's "otherness," waiting for that moment that declares itself as an "event of the Spirit." Such a moment opens us up, amidst all our unresolved questions, to the wonder at the heart of our lives. Spiritual direction is necessarily strongly incarnational and engaged with all of life's ordinariness and materiality, but it has the potential to awaken in us an awareness of the existential quality of God's relationship with all that is. Spiritual direction invites us towards an encounter where, despite all that is seemingly wrong and hurtful in life, a radical and growing sense of the unconditional love of God becomes a genuine possibility.

A basic rule of thumb for spiritual direction is to begin with what *is*, not with what *should be*. To hear God present to us in both the interruptions and circumstances of our lives. Not that God sends us the circumstances to teach us, or to make a point, but the very circumstances we find ourselves in provide the raw material in our everyday life where, as Sarah Bachelard offers, "we find ourselves *addressed*, and

---

4   Chapter Four: First published in *Eremos: Exploring Spirituality in Australia*. April, 2020. Reprinted by permission.

47

addressed, we *find* ourselves" (Bachelard, 36).

There is so much more to us that we often miss. Richard Wilbur's poem "For Dudley" reminds us:

All that we do
Is touched with ocean, yet we remain
On the shore of what we know

—Wilbur (25)

And as Cynthia Bourgeault, in *Centering Prayer and Inner Awakening*, says, "Jesus taught from the conviction that we human beings are victims of a tragic case of mistaken identity" (Bourgeault, 10). I spend so much time and energy on the "little me" that is daily preoccupied and full of anxieties that I take this "little me" to be the "real me," thereby robbing myself of what Thomas Merton would call the True Self (Merton, 32–33). No wonder Merton could say that "Everything has been given to us in Christ. All we need is to experience what we already possess" (Finley, 111). In spiritual direction, we are offered an opportunity to wake up to how we so often stay trapped on "the shore," too frightened even to put our big toe into the ocean. We are also encouraged to listen to the call of that ocean, to realize that even here, in this anxious, preoccupied, never-good-enough place that I am so used to, the ocean—or we might say, Otherness, Love, or the Divine—is constantly addressing me.

So, in the first place, spiritual direction is an act of faith—not so much believing credal statements and asking ourselves constantly "Is all this true?" but instead asking ourselves the very basic question, "Am I true?" As Thomas Merton says, "To work out my own identity in God ... is a labor that requires sacrifice and anguish, risk[s] many tears.... We do not know clearly beforehand what the result of this work will be. The secret of my full identity is hidden in Him. He alone can make me who I am, or rather who I will be when at last I fully begin to be" (Merton 32-3). The faith that is at the heart of spiritual direction is a way of being, referring to something beyond ourselves, waking us up to the depth and mystery at the heart of all things. It is a way of listening, living "in sync" with the "secret call within." It is a way of befriending our desires, our inner truth, and alerting us to live with both freedom and integrity.

There is a lovely poem by American farmer, ecologist, and poet Wendell Berry:

> *The question before me, now that I*
> *am old, is not how to be dead,*
> *which I know from enough practice,*
> *but how to be alive, as these worn*
> *hills still tell, and some paintings*
> *of Paul Cezanne, and this mere*
> *singing wren, who thinks he's alive*
> *forever, this instant, and may be.*

—Berry (222)

The first part of this poem is quoted in Chapter 3 but given in full now because of Berry's wonderful images of "worn hills," "paintings by Cezanne," and "this mere singing wren," that all speak so powerfully, not only to the "rapture of being fully alive," but how grounded such "aliveness" is in our original nature. The great choice set before us in spiritual direction is the perennial one: "I have set before you life and death.... Choose life" (Dt 30:19). One of the great revelations in spiritual direction, and one we need constantly to be reminded of, is how often, in fact, we choose death. We learn, in the things we often bring to spiritual direction, how practiced we are in "how to be dead." We also learn, surprisingly, that it is in this very place of death that we can become alert to the invitation of "how to be alive." It is this little word *how* that is so important in the spiritual director's vocabulary. For the real question is not "Are you saying your prayers?" or "Do you believe the resurrection?" or "Are you going to Church?" but rather "*How* are you living, attending, relating, working, and relaxing now? Is the way you are responding or reacting to your life's circumstances leading you towards freedom and life, or towards addiction, compulsion, and death?"

What Peter Carnley (364) says, in *The Structure of Resurrection Belief*, of the stories of the risen Jesus can surely be said of the gospel stories themselves. For the theological truth of these stories is not so much a propositional truth but a dispositional one. These stories, and Jesus himself, are encouraging us to shift from living according to the rules—always wanting to be orthodox or right and living and believing in a way that stays closed or stuck—towards an attitude or disposition that leads to life and hope. This is why it is important to distinguish in the stories, sayings, and teachings of Jesus that he is not being prescriptive—telling us that we should do this or should be that; rather, he is being descriptive—describing a way of life that leads to life and to freedom.

When Jesus says, "Blessed are the poor in Spirit" he is not suggesting so much that we need to seek poverty, but rather, as Charles Elliott frames it, that you are "in the right place when you are poor" (Elliott, 85). For simply by paying attention to the raw material of our lives, as we are encouraged to do in spiritual direction, we are often confronted with our poverty—our incompleteness, our not knowing, and our failures. Yet it is precisely here that we can discover, in our empty hands and open minds the gift of faith. "Being in the 'right place' implies being poor, gentle, mourning, merciful and peaceable and persecuted—in other words, powerless, weak and vulnerable. How can that possibly be the right place? It is the right place because it makes no claims on anyone, not even on God. And it is then that God's offer of love and wholeness, for the individual and the community, can be accepted. As it is accepted so the richness of the offer is revealed" (Elliott, 86).

But spiritual direction is not only an act of faith, it is also an act of love. Thomas Merton once asked himself, "Who am I?" and he responded, "I am one loved by Christ" (Finley, 96). For he knew, and it is a great gift that we can discover through the ministry of spiritual direction, to realize that it is Christ's transparency, revealing to us his deep loving relationship with the One he called Father, which opens for us the possibility of our participation in that same loving relationship. Made in the image of God, Merton says, we "already have everything, but we don't know it and we don't experience it. Everything has been given to us in Christ. All we need is to experience what we already possess" (Finley, 111). Just as the spiritual director wrestles with her vulnerability and poverty in the surrender of love, offering respectful space to the other who comes for spiritual direction, the directee also struggles to express his own truth and comes to face his own vulnerability and poverty. In this encounter, both spiritual director and directee begin to realize, according to Johannes Baptist Metz, "that the unending nature of our poverty is [our] only innate treasure" (Metz, 29).

The great gift to us in spiritual direction is that it is always relational, always reminding us of the gift of the "other." In the words of Desmond Tutu, "We are persons through other persons" (Tutu, 21). It is vital that as spiritual directors we know this truth—that, as Alan Jones puts it, "I cannot be me without you, and we cannot be us without them" (Jones, 195). This is a deeply liberating experience when an individual becomes a person, when the Trinity, the Community of Love, is experienced, not as a doctrine, but as a lived, living and relational reality.

Once we realize this, we will be able to provide hospitable space for others, and to do this, we can explore the idea of spaciousness. As we provide the space for others, we bear witness that Spirit-Wisdom is not so much the bringer of power but the opener of eyes, and we invite people into that space where it can become possible for them to wake up. In offering space to find their own path, we offer them love. According to Margaret Guenther, "Love impels [our] work and lies at its heart.... [The love of a spiritual director "is a contemplative love, immune from temptation to devour, possess or manipulate" (Guenther, III). The great nineteenth-century spiritual director Friedrich von Hügel told his niece, Gwendolyn Greene, "The golden rule is, to help those we love escape from us" (von Hügel, xxix). For what we are then offering is nothing less than the sacred space of God's gift of life, freedom, and the courage to be.

According to English novelist and philosopher Iris Murdoch, "Love is the extremely difficult realization that something other than oneself is real" (Murdoch, 51). Experiencing the "other" as real involves self-emptying, a kind of poverty of spirit, a self-transcending act. Whenever we are with someone else, that person is not only "other" but also real. Yet imagination does have a part to play in engaging with the reality of another. Just as the imagination is so vitally important in our discovery of self and who we really are, so too is the imagination vital in our relationships. As English novelist Ian McEwan says, "Imagining what it is like to be someone other than yourself is at the core of our humanity. It is the essence of compassion, and the beginning of morality."

Spiritual direction is an act of faith, love, and hope. Hope here is not optimism—not putting our faith in the outcome—but rather realizing that whatever happens, things still make sense in God's larger story. In the face of so much that was wrong in the world and in the human condition, Julian of Norwich could still say, "All will be well, and all will be well, and every kind of thing will be well" (Julian of Norwich, 28). She also reminds us that we are a "marvelous mixture of both well-being and woe," a mixture of good and bad (Julian of Norwich, 52). The emphasis is on *both/and* not on *either/or*. This is why we need in this ministry of spiritual direction what Rowan Williams calls double vision, the "vision of [our] own fear and the vision of the love that overcomes it" (Williams, *What is Christianity?*, 18). This double vision is something we resist, for "it seems as though fear wins," as we face two realities, "unreconciled pain and unexhausted compassion, the history of men and women and the history of God with us" (Williams, *Open*, 55) To have this double vision, we must learn to live with the tension of acknowledging that we live with the *both/and*. As Julian says, "Peace and love are always in us, living and working, but we are not always in peace and love" (Julian of Norwich, 39). Or as Michael Leunig suggests in his well-known prayer, there are only two feelings, "love and fear" (Leunig). We may choose to speak or act from either space because they are both within us.

Julian's great gift to us is to help us see that both are true: "peace and love are always in us," which she calls the higher or absolute truth, *and* "we are not always in peace and love," which she calls the lower or relative truth. She goes on to say, "For we do not fall in the sight of God, and we do not stand in our own sight; and both these are true, as I see it, but the contemplating of our Lord God is the higher truth" (Julian of Norwich, 82). Living with double vision means that while we should not deny or ignore the lower truth, we should never ignore the higher truth. This imaginative insight into the human condition radically transforms how I see both myself and others. In our formation as spiritual directors, it is important that we are encouraged to see ourselves as God sees us, so that the people who come to see us may also begin to see themselves as God sees them.

Jon M. Sweeney and Mark S. Burrows have rendered 14th century mystic and writer Meister Eckhart's thought as poetry:

... not knowing
is the mark of faith

not wanting
the work of hope

and not demanding

53

the gift of love

—Sweeney and Burrows (130)

We do not offer spiritual direction in our own strength, for poverty of spirit is the basic disposition of the spiritual director. We come to this ministry, hopefully well trained and formed, but it is as if we are constantly challenged to put aside what we know, even our strengths, and offer the only gift we can: ourselves. This includes all our vulnerability, weakness, incompleteness, and unknowing. This inner emptiness is the fundamental disposition we need, as we withdraw our hearts from everything that is less than God. This poverty of spirit opens us up to the transforming dispositions of faith and hope and love. We seek to come, just as Jesus came, emptying himself and making space for the other. We attempt to let go of our opinions and our preoccupations and any agenda we might have for ourselves or for those who come to us. We are present to the other, simply trusting that in the silence, space. and freedom we offer, a word of life may be heard. In faith, love, and hope, the spiritual director, in the way she is with the other, mirrors how immediately, intimately, truly, profoundly, passionately, lovingly, and vulnerably God is present, both to the creation and to the whole of humanity.

CHAPTER FIVE

"I believe" because "I am"[5]:
Living More Fully Through My Personal Vocation

*The longest journey
is the journey inwards.*

—Dag Hammarskjöld (65)

Learning to Be Congruent

About eighty years ago in Johannesburg, on the veranda at a woman's hostel, a white man in a flowing black cassock swept past a black woman with a "little black boy of 8 or so" and did what was unthinkable in the South Africa in those days—he doffed his hat to the mother. The boy was Desmond Tutu, and the priest was Fr. Trevor Huddleston. Following Huddleston's death in 1998, Tutu paid tribute to the anti-apartheid bishop at his memorial service:

> I was bowled over that a white man should raise his hat for my mother, a black woman and one who was not even educated. Politically and socially it was unthinkable but Trevor's theology made it natural and unavoidable. He believed fervently in the doctrine that all of us are created in the image of God.

---

5   The title of this chapter comes from H.A. Williams, *Someday I'll Find You*, Collins FountPaperbacks, London, 1982, 1984, 213. "I saw that I could not truly say 'I believe', unless it was another way of saying 'I am.'"

That made us each one not just important but endowed us with infinite worth so that we deserved not just respect but veritable reverence, for each of us then was God's viceroy, God's representative. We were sanctuaries of the Holy Spirit. (Denniston, 269–70)

Trevor Huddleston became famous as a champion in the fight against apartheid in South Africa and celebrated throughout the world with his book *Naught for Your Comfort*. Among other things he said, "You cannot love an abstraction" and "The only chosen race is the human race." He lived from the inside out, his actions emanating out of a sustained way of seeing things, a controlling vision. Such a vision acts as an interpretative lens, which allows a person not only to see the attitudes and actions that mark his life but also to live congruently, such that one's life becomes a natural embodiment of that vision, what Donald McKinnon identifies as "the inevitable consequence of a persistent religious fidelity" (McGrandle, 209).

The God of Jesus: "Never...more divine than in this humanity"

The gospels are remarkably consistent on one aspect of the identity and mission of Jesus. Behind his wonderful works and wise words is a person, who invites us to enter into his way of life and self-giving love by becoming participants in his inner experience. For the focus of the gospels is the character of Jesus, and character is not so much what we do but the way we do it. Jesus's experience was marked by a deep interior silence, and the richness and depth of his extraordinary capacity for his relationship with God was a profound mark of his self-knowledge and his personal authority. For the true miracle of this man, Jesus of Nazareth, was the way he was with others. Jesus, as Rowan Williams said, did "not do miracles to prove a point," for "the point is that the miracle is not the point" (Williams, *Meeting God*, 34).

As Simone Weil saw so clearly, "When [compassion for the afflicted] is really found we have a more astonishing miracle than walking on water, healing the sick, or even raising the dead" (Weil, 79). He knew he was both seen and heard by God, spoken to in the nakedness of personal encounter, so he was able to be with people in such a way that they too found themselves as what Hans Urs von Balthasar calls "hearers of the Word" and in responding to the Word discovered their "full dignity" as human beings (Balthasar, 18–19). Our deepest need is to be seen and heard, to be taken seriously, and the way Jesus could stand still, look, listen, and wait upon others was enough to elicit in them their deepest needs or desires.

What we have learned in the twentieth century, through therapy— something that Jesus demonstrated so powerfully in his ministry—is that the crucial element in the relationship between therapist and client is the self-knowledge and self-acceptance of the therapist. This is, of course, true as well for the relationship between the spiritual director and the directee. In Jesus, we see a person who was so deeply immersed in the God whom he called Father that God lived fully in union with Jesus, so that his life was characterized by an unconditional and radically selfless love towards others. Jesus, knowing that he was loved to the core of his being, lived his humanity truly and freely, vulnerably, and fruitfully. For him, self-knowledge was his central and abiding truth.

This can be seen throughout the gospels and was something he grasped in faith and sustained in prayer. Tested again and again, it found its ultimate expression in the movement from action to passion, graphically demonstrated in the cross as the power of vulnerable love. This is not so much conceptual knowledge, but the experiential knowledge born out of self-surrender and love, not knowing so much as being loved. This knowledge is about accepting the fact that we are·accepted, beloved by God. The people who encountered Jesus somehow felt drawn into the "force-field" of his beloved-ness. The way Jesus was with others, and the very character of his life and passion, challenges our conventional view of God, the God of Jesus. As Jürgen Moltmann saw, "God is not more glorious than he is in this self-surrender ... nor more divine than he is in this humanity" (Moltmann, 205).

***

Over thirty years ago, when I was doing my initial formation in spiritual direction, it was suggested to me that I could ask myself a couple of key questions—questions that could prove useful in my practice with people coming for spiritual direction. The first question is "What are three words that describe how you see God?" When you have thought about that for a while, and come up with three words, follow with the next question: "What are three words that describe how God sees you?" In my experience over these past thirty years, it is the second question that usually stops us in our tracks.

The first question is relatively easy, in that it does not really cost us anything. It is a question about "out there," so most of us can come up with words like creator, love *or* forgiving. *All good words, but it is the second question that has a bit of a hook in it. For it is an "inside" kind of question that catches and involves me, for I am a part of the answer. This question puts me directly on the line, asking me to get in touch with my everyday lived experience, to get in touch with my truth. The second question opens most of us up to a bit of a gap between what I (perhaps too easily) profess and my lived experience. Not that I think that this gap is terminal—it need not be the end of the world. This gap, if you like, can be precisely the place— the place of self-knowledge—where grace can speak into!*

***

"My task now is to become a human being"

Jesus lived his humanity out of his self-knowledge, and his gift to us is that we too can live, accepting ourselves as people who do not belong to themselves. Like him, we are not autonomous, isolated individuals but rather persons-in-relation, with an inherent capacity for the infinite, able to participate in the inner experience that shaped his consciousness and helps us become aware that the Divine Spirit is the true subject of our being. So, with St. Paul in Ga 2:20, we can say, "It is no longer I who live, but it is Christ who lives in me." The humanity of Jesus holds up to us a transformative vision of what it is to be human. Because we are human, we are possessed of an intrinsic and inviolable dignity.

The secret Jesus offers us is not, as we perhaps too often think, a particular way of being religious, but a universal way of being human, living the gift of being able to say, "I am," or as Rabbi Abraham Heschel puts it, "I was born ... and my task now is to become a human being" (O'Leary, 105). The truth is that most of us need to revision ourselves daily; we need an attractive, imaginative, and often alternative image of our self so that we can live freely and well. It was out of the experience of the destruction by the atomic bomb in Hiroshima on the Feast of the Transfiguration in 1945 that Jesuit priest Pedro Arrupe could say, "When will humanity discover that in the core of people there lives the divine reality?"

Who we are and who I am are profoundly crucial in the ministry of spiritual direction. We forget that the primary instrument of ministry is our own fragile selves. Alan Jones vulnerably expresses this: "With us who are consciously responding to a call to be a companion, the medium is the message. We cannot genuinely *talk* about companioning without *being* a companion. We are a word about the word. We are not to offer dogma, we are to offer ourselves" (Jones, 39). This is why Benedict XVI said that "in addition to their necessary professional training" charity workers need a "formation of the heart," so that they may be "led to that encounter with God in Christ which awakens their love and opens their spirits to others" (Benedict XVI, 53). Margaret Guenther was committed to the ongoing professional skills and development of spiritual directors yet said that "The amateur is the one who loves, loves the art and those she serves, loves and prays for the people who trust her, loves the Holy Spirit who is the true Director in this strange ministry called spiritual direction" (Guenther, 1). Clearly, we need skills and knowledge, but our ministry must be grounded in the call of the Holy Spirit and confirmed by the community of faith. It is this paradox that offers us balance and lies at the heart of our vocation.

"Love is the epiphany of God in our poverty" —Thomas Merton (Finley, 97)

Claiming and acting on this truth about ourselves is not always easy. We are only too aware of our fear of failure and a sense of inadequacy. Such unknowing, emptiness, and poverty of spirit is not something we acquire. We truly "possess" this radical poverty as a "given," but only when we learn to forget ourselves and accept this larger truth about ourselves. We do not offer spiritual direction in our own strength. Hopefully, we come to this ministry well-trained and formed, yet we are constantly challenged to put aside what we know, even our strengths, to offer the only gift we can: ourselves—vulnerable, weak, incomplete, and unknowing. Here, we can make space for the other, attempting to let go of our opinions, preoccupations, projects, illusions, judgments, and agendas that we might have for ourselves and for those coming to see us. This offering of space is indeed an act of love. This vulnerable and respectful offering of safe space is a gift for the other. We come to spiritual direction to be simply present in this space, trusting that in this silence and space we might both experience a freedom in which a primordial word is heard. This is the basic paradox of this ministry, and it is only by acknowledging and accepting our poverty that we will discover our worth and our truth wealth. The wound of self-knowledge is the way forward, if only we can accept this truth. In the Australian poet Kevin Hart's words, "I come to wound you and to heal the wound" (Hart, 87).

Thomas Merton offers a warning to those in ministry: "He who attempts to act and do things for others or for the world without deepening his own self-understanding, freedom, integrity, and capacity to love, will not have anything to give others. He will communicate to them nothing but the contagion of his own obsessions, his aggressiveness, his ego-centered ambitions, his delusions about ends and means, his doctrinaire prejudices and ideas" (Merton, *Contemplation*, 160-1). Merton also says words that not only emphasize that such poverty is the right place, but that it is a very fertile place for compassion. "My fall into inconsistency was nothing but the revelation of what I am... I am thrown into contradiction: to realize it is mercy, to accept it is love, to help others do the same is compassion" (Merton, *Learning to Love*, 106, 355). Is there a better description of the power and gift of self-knowledge that the spiritual director offers those coming for spiritual direction?

***

I was staring at a very bleak future, now over twenty-five years ago. I found myself telling my spiritual director at the time just how bad I felt, to which she said I was in a privileged place. I could not believe my ears. Privileged place!? "Yes," she said, "privileged because this is an invitation into sharing in the paschal mystery." I exploded. "I'm happy to preach the paschal mystery, but I don't want to live it!" It was in a flash that I knew I had spoken not only an untruth—'I don't want to live it!'—but a previously unacknowledged profound truth. It was then, as I came to reflect on it, that I realized that this is in many ways the very essence of spiritual direction. As we try to express what is on our hearts and minds, being as real as we possibly can, we wake up to what it is that is most deeply who we are and what we most deeply want. Or as Denys Turner proclaimed, "What we most truly want is what we most really are" (Turner, 204).

***

61

The crisis comes when we begin to realize that we are victims of a mistaken identity. The self that I normally take myself to be, preoccupied and anxious, is only a small part of who I really am. If I try to seek fulfillment at this level, I will miss out on the bigger life that is on offer. No wonder Jesus, through his personal insight, could in Mt 10:39 say, "Those who find their life will lose it, and those who lose their life for my sake will find it." Ronald Rolheiser offers an image of each soul before we are born, kissed and caressed by God, hidden in our memory, that becomes a lens through which we live all our lives. Jesus not only tells us something about God, but he also offers us an expansive vision of what it is to be human.

As we saw in the previous chapter, everything is already ours, but we just do not know it or even experience it. One of the great gifts spiritual direction can offer is what Thomas Merton says is the encouragement "to giving ourselves in prayer a chance to realize that we have what we seek. We don't have to rush after it. It is there all the time, and if we give it time it will make itself known to us" (de Waal 17-8). As spiritual directors, we need both grace and discipline. We are, as Carolyn Gratton describes, "value bearers who are good for the other and also value concealers whose own needs and distortion of reality may have a negative effect. The grace and discipline we need is to recognize this truth about ourselves so that we can be an authentic presence for the other in a way that they too discover and live out of the truth about themselves" We need to be steadily distanced from our own, and the seeker's drives, needs and passions, so that we can authentically represent the demand of grace and Otherness" (Gratton, *Guidelines*, 185-6).

My Personal Vocation: To Be Myself

When it comes to thinking about vocation, we need to be clear. There is the call to follow Jesus, there is the call to an other-directed role, and there is, crucially, the call to be ourselves. Words often get hijacked, and *vocation* is one such word where the personal dimension of call is often hidden, ignored, or diminished. What we have seen in the experience of Jesus is that vocation is rightly about both origin and destiny and not just about "who we are" but also "whose we are." Walter Bruggeman suggests that it is about finding a "purpose for being in the world that is related to the purposes of God" (Gratton, *The Art*, 157). We have already seen that, made in the image of God, we naturally reflect the relational, mutual Community of Love, or the Trinity. Being human does not exist in the solitary affirmation of our individual autonomy but rather in our availability and receptivity. Rowan Williams is clear: "In the most basic sense of all, God's call is to *be*: the vocation of creatures is to exist. And, secondly, the vocation of creatures is to exist as *themselves*, to be bearers of their names, answering to the word which gives each its distinctive identity" (Williams, *Open*, 173).

Vocation derives from the Latin word *vox*, so vocation has to do with being addressed by a voice—a deeply personal voice saying, "You shall be my people, and I will be your God" (Jer. 30:22). Our personal call, when properly attended to, will act as a "strange attractor," drawing together and integrating all the varying elements of our life so that we can live congruently and with purpose and integrity. Human beings are made in the image of God, and Jesus transparently shows us through his inner experience that we too can access an interpersonal relationship with God's self. We are both being addressed by God as "Thou" and responsible before God as "I."

Miriam Rose Ungunmerr-Baumann, an Indigenous woman, author of *Dadirri*, and Senior Australian of the Year 2021, wrote, "I am beginning to hear the gospel at the level of my identity" (Ungunmerr-Baumann, 1-4). Knowledge of God is inextricably bound up with knowledge of ourselves, so rather than spending all our time asking whether the doctrines of the Church or the Bible are true, our time will be well spent facing the real question that they both pose: "Am I true?" In this way, I can begin to find the courage to become what I already am, which is about feeling at home with oneself—*e* grounded, and knowing where I am, where I have come f where am I going. This is the place to be, for as it has been said, "God is not elsewhere." In this "karaoke society" of ours, where we are too often tempted to sing someone else's song, we can hopefully learn to sing our own song, and be in touch with the rhythm within, realizing both our own giftedness and beloved-ness (Williams, *Open*, 176). Just before being hanged in prison, Dietrich Bonhoeffer wrote this poem:

Who am I? This or the other?
Am I one person today and tomorrow another?
Am I both at once? A hypocrite before others,
And before myself a contemptibly woebegone weakling?...

Who am I? They mock me, these lonely questions of mine,
Whoever I am, thou knowest, O God, I am thine!

—Bonhoeffer (173)

***

One's personal relationship with God is paramount in our vocation to be a spiritual director, and what the person coming into spiritual direction needs is not so much insight as an encounter with the living God. So it is that the spiritual director, and the gift she brings, is her own encounter with God. I well remember, many years ago, when I was a very young priest in my first parish, meeting with a man who was an alcoholic. I got to know him, and I vividly remember one day when he sat with me in my study. He was very drunk, but being both young and naïve, I continued the conversation. It was inevitably very frustrating, and in exasperation I wanted to say that he was hopeless. He stopped me mid-sentence and said, in his drunken drawl, "Fr. Philip, you are a priest, and if you say I am hopeless, you are in a worse place that I am." I have never forgotten that encounter. Rarely can I say that God has spoken to me so directly as on that occasion. It has been one of the most precious gifts in my ministry.

***

"Love is my name"

To really exist is to exist as responding to God, responding, each of us, in a uniquely different way. Rowan Williams says that we are to mirror God, that our personal vocation is to find our own way of playing back to God his self-caring, self-losing care and compassion (Williams, *Open*, 175). This is the task our personal vocation sets us to discover and live out what I alone can reflect from God's goodness and love. To do this, we need to be real, to feel at home, and to be grounded—just as God asked Adam in the Garden, "Where are you?" It is as if God endlessly asks us the same question, not for his sake so much as for ours. "Here I am" becomes the human response, yet to stay here, to know this is the right place, is not necessarily easy.

As Thomas Merton says, "To work out my own identity in God ... is a labor that requires sacrifice and anguish, risk, and many tears. I do not know clearly beforehand what the result of this work will be, the secret of my full identity is hidden in him. He alone can make me who I am, or rather who I will be when at last I fully begin to be" (Merton, *New Seeds*, 32–33). For Merton, just as it was for his favorite English theologian, Julian of Norwich, Love was both God's meaning and ours. "To say that I am made in the image of God is to say that love is the reason for my existence, for God is love. Love is my true identity. Self-lessness is my true self. Love is my true character. Love is my name" (Merton, *Contemplation*, 60).

"Vocation is...when all the games have stopped"

Rowan Williams says that "Vocation has to do with saving your soul—not by acquiring a secure position of holiness, but by learning to shed the unreality which simply suffocates the very life of the soul.... *Vocation is, you could say, what's left when all the games have stopped* [emphasis added] (Williams, *Open*, 176). All this has profound implications for the ministry of spiritual direction—for both the spiritual director and directee. This shedding of "the unreality which simply suffocates the very life of the soul" opens us up to the vulnerability of facing our truth, which, according to Jesus, is "poverty of spirit," where we can experience the truth, as Paul saw, that "My grace is sufficient for you, for my power is made perfect in weakness" (2 Cor. 12:9).

The crisis where we begin to wake up to the truth, that this poverty of spirit is the right place for me, occurs when we realize that God cannot reach me if I am not there. This suggests that sin is fundamentally our refusal to be who we are or seeing our life through someone else's eyes. Finding our unique way of being ourselves means facing the games we so often play, the unreality of our selfish, self-protecting illusions, our struggles for cheap security, all of which blocks this call to be ourselves. The temptation to live like that may offer some safety, but it is not true, and it is not me. To find the space to be ourselves, to stop hiding and to be simply who we are, even in our weakness, poverty, and vulnerability, is the spaciousness and freedom of what the Christian tradition has always called salvation. It is the ability to be transparent through honesty and self-acceptance and live with freedom and openness. This is the great gift that spiritual direction can bring. As I have said elsewhere, spiritual direction is a gifted presence to help a gifted self emerge.

God, in Jesus, has not only said "Yes" to humanity and creation but, in the same Jesus, humanity and creation have said "Yes" to God. It is as if Jesus is affirming our original nature. Our life, limited and fragmented in so many ways, limited as Jesus's life also was, is simply about responding to *this* Jesus, the "human image of divinity, and divine image of humanity," by joining our "yes" to his "Yes." The best way to do that is to claim for ourselves our personal vocation. Being ourselves, singing our own song, being in touch with the rhythm within, celebrating our gifts, while all the while acknowledging our limitations and even our weaknesses, seeing them not as defects but the other side of our gifts. Then we will have the courage and the freedom to mirror and reflect something of the diversity and richness of God.

PART II

"The discernment of spirits which is called for is an entrance into an understanding of a language of God spoken within our very being."

—Ignatius of Loyola (107)

CHAPTER SIX

Choosing Life:
The Journey Towards Discernment

Decision making is an intrinsic part of being human, ranging from everyday, spontaneous, and even unreflective decisions to those that are the result of much consideration and, for many of us, prayer. In fact, decisions are a requisite of life, and all of them have consequences. The decisions we make determine whether we live authentically, in keeping with our own sense of who we are as people, or not, and whether we become more, or less, fully human and fully alive. Choosing life is both a simple and profound choice facing us all, and the process that enables us to do so is one of discernment, through careful attention, not only to the way we make our decisions but also to the fruit of the decisions we make. This process is done within the context of our everyday lived experiences, our joys and sorrows, our hopes and losses, our relationships, our work, and our personal interests. For many committed to living both deeply and authentically, one of the ways to facilitate this process is to commit to an ongoing relationship with a spiritual director or companion. This chapter looks at five paths each of us can follow to make life-enhancing and life-changing decisions. Each section ends by looking at the way the spiritual director needs to be committed to her own discernment process and vocation, living and practicing the ministry of spiritual direction in order to demonstrate an authentic and effective means of facilitating grace for those who come to see her.

Discernment is a gift at the heart of Christian discipleship. It is the practical and practiced way of living as congruently as possible in the way of Jesus. It is learning to respond in love to God, to others, to our world, and to our circumstances. It is a habit of faith, where all is grace, yet, in the economy of God's grace, there is always the responsive and crucial role of human action. It is neither an accomplishment nor an achievement, nor an end in itself, but it is rather a never-ending journey, pointing to and growing into the transformative love of God.

It is fundamentally about paying attention and becoming more aware of the movement and action of the Spirit of God. It is not problem solving or having an opinion. It is neither about discovering some unknown part of God's plan nor about getting everything right, so much as it is being in tune with the music and the dance of God. Discernment is often defined as "comprehending the will of God" and the consequent desire to live congruently with that will. It is helpful to think about that in the context of God's hope and desires for us, realizing with Julian of Norwich that "Love is our Lord's meaning" (Julian, 86) and that God wants us to participate in and cooperate with God's vision for the whole of creation. Therefore, discernment is something worked out in the actuality of everyday life and in the changes and chances of our worldly experience, where we discover the activity and invitation of the Spirit of God. It is not theoretical knowledge. It is not necessarily "fail-safe." It is, as some say, "wisdom won at the risk of error," where nothing is wasted.

Discernment shapes and forms us so that we gradually grow into the "likeness of Christ," and it is where, as it is said in Phil 2:5, 1 Cor. 2:16, we "put on the mind of Christ." Discernment is about allowing our deepest values and aspirations to come to the surface as we sift through what is genuine or true and what is false. It is about discriminating or distinguishing between two paths, as in the book of Deuteronomy (30:15, 19) where God says, "I have set before you life and prosperity, death and adversity.... Choose life."

As we pay attention to the raw material of our everyday life, we notice "movements" within us—movements of peace or turmoil, of attractions or revulsions. Noticing these two ways, learning to make choices in freedom so that we are no longer hijacked by any disordered love or attachment, and beginning to accept, welcome, and desire whatever God wants, are all part of discernment.

Disposition: The Way I Am

Friedrich von Hügel, the eminent nineteenth-century spiritual director, wrote to his niece that "Dispositions are the means to acquiring reality" (von Hügel,14). By dispositions, he meant our capacity to be open, aware, and truthful. Prayer, then, which has at its heart discernment, is not only a matter of attention but also *intention*, where we dispose ourselves to recognize what God is offering us, and, in Ignatius of Loyola's words, placing "myself before God in reverence... [begging] him to direct everything in my day more and more to his service and praise" (Fleming, 91). What matters, as the Christian tradition maintains, is that our spiritual and emotional health rests not on what happens to us, or the circumstances we find ourselves in, but rather on *how we respond* to what happens to us.

Ronald Rolheiser writes, "Long before we do anything explicitly religious at all, we have to do something about the fire that burns within us. What we do with that fire, how we channel it, is our spirituality.... And how we do channel it, the disciplines and habits we choose to live by, will either lead to a greater integration or disintegration within our bodies, minds, and souls" (Rolheiser, 6,11). As Ignatius of Loyola saw, "The discernment of spirits which is called for is an entrance into understanding a language of God spoken within our very being" (Fleming, 176). Made in the image of God, it is in the very fabric of our being, in our attitudes towards the very circumstances of our lives, where we can both notice and respond to God. But as many writers have said, discernment is not principally about the morality of good or bad actions, nor is it a kind of blueprint that bears no relation to who we really are, and neither is it about finding the "right" solution to a puzzle. It is more like being given a set of building blocks and engaging them with commitment, intelligence, and care.

As human beings, we are not isolated individuals but rather persons-in-relation, so we are not alone in our task of sifting through the "given-ness" of our personal and communal lives. The disposition of openness that helps us align with reality suggests that not only the Divine Other but also all the others in our lives can throw light on our quest for both the truth and the courage to choose and live out of that truth. As the tradition has always maintained, self-knowledge is intimately linked to the knowledge of God. This call to our inner truth is our vocation; as Frederick Buechner said, "The place where God calls you to is the place where your deep gladness and the world's deep hunger meet" (Buechner, 95). The gift of discernment confronts us. Our choices matter—for ourselves, and for the wider community, and in fact the whole of creation.

Subsequently, the questions I need to ask myself are, "Where am I? And what is going on for me at present?" This suggests that I must try (without judgment) to be in touch with the things I cannot change— my natural family, genetic makeup, place and culture of birth, up-bringing, education, circumstances, giftedness, shortcomings, health, disabilities, and the like. Then I need to ask, how am I at present? How am I living with the mystery, with the fire? What is the attitude (reflected in my choices) that I bring to life? And can I get in touch with times in my life when I have been tempted simply to change the *where* in my life (in other words, to change my circumstances) instead of changing my attitude? Have I sometimes simply moved or shifted the circumstances of my life, hoping that that will make a difference?

Initially, one of the tasks of the spiritual director is to assess the readiness of the one coming for direction, or at least his desire to proceed. The spiritual director will listen respectfully, and with encouragement, by affirming in her directee his own sense of personal worth, and through these attitudes of approach help clarify his sense of what is going on in his life, what is significant in terms of natural giftedness and the invitation of grace, and what is helpful or unhelpful in his basic attitude towards life. The manner in which the spiritual director is available to the other is of paramount importance, reflecting in many ways the transformative power in the way Jesus was available to others.

Detachment: The Way of Freedom

Our disciplines of attending are about noticing what our hearts run after—our disordered longings that move us away from God and lock us into self-defeating and destructive ways of living. It is always helpful to ask ourselves where a particular mood, feeling, behavior, or action leads. However important the root cause of such moods, feelings, and behaviors are, it is vital that we focus on the direction our desires and longings are moving.

Ignatius said, "we must be so poised [detached/indifferent] that we do not cling to any created thing as though it were our ultimate good, but remain open to the possibility that love may demand of us poverty rather than riches, sickness rather than health, dishonour rather than honour, a short life rather than a long one, because God alone is our security, refuge and strength" (Hughes, 63). Ignatian "indifference" must not be confused with our everyday understanding of indifference as uncaring, lacking any attachments, and impartial. The Ignatian understanding of "indifference" means that we are as free as possible to follow the will of God. As such, it requires passion to overcome addictions, compulsions, and inordinate desires of all kinds, and such indifference actually channels such passion towards that which ultimately satisfies and fulfills us more. We grow into spiritual freedom, as Ignatius says, "by gradually bringing an order of values into our lives so that we make no choice or decisions because we have been influenced by some disordered attachment or love" (Fleming, 21).

Monica Furlong says of God in her arresting poem, "Attracting":

Fatally attracting
Our waywardness
Into new tracks
Of faithfulness.

—Furlong (72)

In other words, do I dare to be "fatally attracted?" Do I know, and can I count, the cost? Am I willing to "let go and let God," in who's service is perfect freedom? This is the freedom that detachment can bring, or what Ignatius called indifference. He said, "We can be so detached from any created thing only if we have a stronger attachment" and this can happen only if "our one dominating desire and fundamental choice must be to live in love in [God's] presence" (Hughes 23). We have already seen that attention, or attentiveness, is crucial, but we must also consider and integrate our *intention*, and Ignatius teaches that *purity of intention* is vital.

While the natural and learned skills the spiritual director brings to the encounter are very important, what is critical is our own sense of personal freedom, not the least of which are awareness and desire for freedom from our illusions, prejudices, projections, and fears. It is our own sense of personal freedom and being beloved that allows us to pay attention to the one coming for direction with the utmost respect and compassion. The willingness to put aside our own opinions, ideas, and expectations, to provide the best possible environment and space where the other, perhaps for the first time, not only begins to hear herself, getting in touch with her own history of freedom and constraint, but also begins to see the fruit of the decisions she has made in the past, is our unique gift.

Dream: The Way I Imagine

One of our besetting problems is that we too often devalue the imagination. Yet imagination is crucial for the life God calls us to. For too long we have devalued the imagination and relegated it to the merely imaginary, fantasy, or make-believe. Our imaginations reveal an unseen level of inner reality. When our imaginations are blocked and we have forgotten the power of story, image, symbol, and poetry, we can so easily become vulnerable to despair.

Imagination is crucial for the life God calls us to. It makes connections for us, between our experience and the texts and stories of our tradition. We are image makers and image bearers, made as we are, in the image of God. We have a remarkable ability to form and be formed by images. We can grasp and deal with reality through our imaginations—through story, poetry, pictures, and symbols—and, as a result, are able to grasp the true and the real far more effectively than intellect or reason ever can.

Thomas Merton says that the imagination is a "discovering faculty, a faculty for seeing relationships, for seeing meanings that are special and even quite new" (de Waal, 23). And Shakespeare mused in *A Midsummer Night's Dream* that "imagination bodies forth the forms of things/unknown" (Act V, Scene I). It enlarges our hearts and our vision, enabling us to see more clearly into alternative and attractive possibilities that we could scarcely dream of without it. Jesus, of course, was a highly imaginative person. His vision of the Kingdom or Reign of God, the centerpiece of his teaching, is a creative, alternative, and attractive image of reality.

Jesus offered parables to open us up to a new way of seeing things and to jolt us into seeing what our hearts so often run after. The Kingdom parable of the treasure hidden in a field in Mt 13:44 asks of us, where and what is my treasure? Where am I investing my time, thoughts, and resources? What excites me and gives me energy for life? Luke's Jesus similarly proclaims: "For where your treasure is, there your heart will be also" (Lk 12:34).

Matthew's story of the Kingdom, which he says is "like a merchant looking for fine pearls," (Mt 12:45) confronts us is with questions such as, what does it feel like to be found, and to be discovered and named as a 'pearl'? How hard has it been, or how hard is it for me to live out of this extraordinarily gifted place where we are the pearls, found by the Kingdom of God? And are we allowing our imaginations to stimulate or encourage me to be in touch with and live out of my deepest desires?

In many respects, because we have undervalued the importance of the imagination, one of the principal gifts a spiritual director brings to the rela-

tionship is the capacity to nurture the imaginative faculty in the one coming for direction. This can only happen if the spiritual director's own life is sustained by a lived experience of the power of story and images, metaphor and parable, and the wonder at the heart of our own sacramental appreciation of our world. One of the best ways to encourage a spiritual directee's appreciation of their imaginative life is by way of indirection, of gently asking what it is that fills them with wonder, or a sense of relaxed enjoyment, be it walking, gardening, music, art, reading, silence, dance, or making connections.

Desire: The Way I Want

As we begin to identify our desires, we realize that God is not so much "out there" but rather "in here." Our vocation, seen in the Word made flesh in Jesus of Nazareth, is to become fully alive, fully human. Jesus is the very truth of our existence. We become aware, as Ignatius did, that the Divine Spirit is the true subject of our being, waking up to how God desires us as God desires God, in the Community or Trinity of Love. So, prayer is literally "owning up" to our innate poverty of Spirit, our inability to pray, and a recognition and acceptance that God is the one who lives and prays in us! Ann and Barry Ulanov describe prayer as "the place where we sort out our desires and where we are ourselves sorted out by the desires we choose to follow" (Ulanov and Ulanov, 20).

In *The God of Surprises*, Gerard Hughes says that "the saint is the person who has discovered his or her deepest desire" (Hughes, 62). He suggests an interesting and helpful exercise. He invites us to spend some time writing the kind of obituary that, in your wildest dreams, you would love to have. We should not try to analyze it, or try to think it out too clearly, but rather allow our fancy to run free. As we do this, we may become aware of those things in our life that are destructive, lead nowhere, are negative and deadening, or block, inhibit, rob, or starve us of life. These movements are often characterized by fear or anxiety. Now we can listen for another movement within, often unnoticed and drowned out by stronger, more insistent negative voices. This is the movement towards life and, if given room, is full of life, promise, hope, energy, and purpose.

Helping a person to get in touch with his desires often results in simultaneous feelings of both vulnerability and excitement. The Christian spiritual director, being present to the other, and recognizing their own lived history of desire, including the wrong routes that have sometimes been involved, has the opportunity of opening up for the one coming to direction a more expansive and deeper appreciation of God, a God made known to us through the Paschal Mystery of Jesus, a God made known to us preeminently through vulnerability, weakness, and self-emptying love. This expanding appreciation of who God really is, and who we really are, flourishing only when we give ourselves away in love, requires both patience and sensitivity on the part of the spiritual director.

Decision: The Way I Choose

The gospel is both gift and task, offering us a vision where everything has already been done. The Kingdom is among us, Jesus has been raised, and we've "got a job to do." Without that initial impetus of the "given," however, that astonishing moment of realization that all is grace, undeserved yet true, the best will in the world is merely effort. As we get in touch with the desire of our hearts, we begin to realize that change in ourselves and in our world is what we want and need. The touch of grace, together with the opening up of a vision of an alternative, imaginative, and attractive possibility, leads us to realize that we can, as Gandhi said, become "the change that [we] wish to see in the world."

It is here that we realize that discernment, and the fruit of that discernment, lies in the decisions and choices we make, and that such choices and decisions are not simply "things to do" but are rather a way of being that is inextricably part of our very being, having to do with our vocation and our identity. If we want God to be real, we must be real ourselves, shedding the unreality that too often clouds our vision and, as Rowan Williams says, "suffocates our soul" (Williams, 176). Deliberately and intentionally, we must pay attention to the movements of our hearts—movements that either lead us to a greater integration or disintegration in our lives, movements that lead either to life or to death.

David Ford's comment that discernment is about "the long-term shaping of our lives by desires that we *own*" further encourages us to shift our attention from "out there," though a necessary first move, to "in here," realizing that we are incomplete and unfinished as human beings, and that properly speaking, we are "human becomings" (Ford, 96). All is grace, but there is work to do and it begins with me. Our responses matter. Are we able to proclaim with Ignatius, "I ask of our Lord that I might be able to hear his call, and that I might be ready and willing to do what he wants" (Fleming, 91)?

This call and response within ourselves may begin with questions such as: What are the key temptations in my life and what happens within me when I allow myself to be controlled by them and therefore robbed of choice? Can I look at the choices I have made in the past, and see how they have shaped or formed my present self? What choices present themselves to me now and where will they lead? How prepared am I to be more and more shaped into the likeness of Christ? How willing am I to be vulnerable and unprotected before God? Or to consider poverty, weakness, and unpopularity? Do I welcome or avoid these attitudes and states Jesus calls "blessed"? As I grow in awareness of the struggle within me between different sets of values and types of wisdoms, can I hear an invitation towards a radical conversion of outlook and a growing freedom to desire the grace to live as Christ lived?

Addressing these questions, the spiritual director begins to realize, often quite profoundly, that her role has been that of the midwife, where someone is birthed into new life. The midwife accompanies a woman giving birth, encouraging her, and reassuring her through a profound and painful process. The midwife brings her skills and compassion to the great mystery of birth.

She has not created this situation but attends and listens, ever vigilant and poised, offering a safe space and a very human face for the miracle of birth. She is free to help the new mother see both the gift and the opportunity of new life that is hers to embrace and nurture. Faced with a growing sense of wonder at the natural world and his own being, the one seeking spiritual direction can begin to feel a certain personal empowerment that is nothing less than the responsibility of growing up, imbued with a sense of wholeness and a growing realization of the coming to fulfillment of his personal vocation and the importance of choice in the call to be both fully alive and fully human.

***

Simone Weil says that "attention animated by desire is the whole foundation of religious practices" (Weil, 150). As we have seen, our *disposition* or attitude is crucial to discernment. Paying attention, we notice inner and often hidden movements within us, movements toward both peace and turmoil. In attending to these movements, we can learn to seek liberation from what is harmful, and in this new-found freedom we can discover, through *detachment*, an even greater attachment. Then, through our *imagination*, we wake up to what might be, to what is not yet, and envision an alternative, imaginative, and attractive way of being and living. We begin to tap into our deepest *desires* and so find the courage to make life-affirming, life-enhancing, and life-transforming *choices*.

CHAPTER SEVEN

A "thinking heart": How Reflecting Theologically Is Integral to the Practice of Spiritual Direction

Etty Hillesum, a twenty-seven-year-old Jewish woman from Amsterdam, died in Auschwitz on November 30, 1943. Throughout the descent into Nazism, she kept an extraordinarily moving diary, addressing "that deeper and wider part [of herself] in which I repose ... what I call 'God'" (Hillesum, 245).

"At night, as I lay in the camp on my plank bed, surrounded by women and girls gently snoring, dreaming aloud, quietly sobbing and tossing and turning, women and girls who often told me during the day, 'We don't want to think, we don't want to feel, otherwise we are sure to go out of our minds,' I was sometimes filled with an infinite tenderness, and lay awake for hours letting all the many, too many impressions of a much too long day wash over me, and I prayed, 'Let me be the thinking heart of these barracks.' And that is what I want to be again. The thinking heart of a whole concentration camp" (Hillesum, 245). Etty prays for a *"thinking heart"*—she wants to think *and* to feel, to bring together both head and heart.

In many ways, we are heirs to a domineering way of practicing theology, which has been either too rational or speculative, revealing a split between head and heart, theology and spirituality. Thomas Merton was deeply attracted to the expressions of Julian of Norwich, whom he saw as a "wise heart" (Merton, *Conjectures*, 211-12) and saw in her a rediscovery of something that could heal this centuries-long "dissociation of sensibility." Merton recognized in her "a true theologian with greater clarity, depth, and order than St. Teresa.... Julian is with Newman, the greatest English theologian." Of her theological method, Merton writes, "She first experienced, then thought, and the thoughtful deepening of experience worked it back into her life, deeper and deeper." For Merton, the heart of Julian's theology was not "solving the contradiction, but remaining in the midst of it, in peace, knowing that it is fully solved, but that the solution is secret, and will never be guessed until it is revealed" (Merton, *Conjectures*, 211-12).

Theology and Spirituality

What we have been witnessing over the past few decades is a shift towards a new consciousness, where we are valuing once more a retrieval of the mystical element of Christianity. In this retrieval, we "discover ... and deepen what [we] already have ... [and] experience what we already possess," as Merton says (Finley, III). Here, we experience a "hidden wholeness" (Merton, *Collected Poems*, 363), in the point of convergence which is sometimes called "the cave of the heart". This consciousness, old yet new, is marked by an interior conversion of heart, an awakening of the contemplative spirit, a radical vulnerability and openness to transcendental reality, and a realization that truth is apprehended not by the mind but by the heart. Harvey Cox suggests that if we could call the first two centuries of Christian life the Age of Faith, a following of the Way of Jesus, which was enlivened by the Spirit of God, then the next several centuries could be called the Age of Belief. This has been an age of creeds, doctrines, and increasing control, hierarchy, and authority. The new consciousness, into which we are moving in our own lifetime, he suggests, could be called the Age of the Spirit, a return to the early church's inspiration, but not a repetition of it (Cox, 4–9).

The deep connection between theology and prayer, which Evagrius of Pontica expressed in his statement that a "theologian is one whose prayer is true" (Clément, 84), was reclaimed by William Temple, a former archbishop of Canterbury in the 1940s, when he saw worship or liturgical prayer as the "quickening of conscience by [God's] holiness; the nourishment of mind with [God's] truth; the purification of imagination by [God's] beauty; the opening of the heart to [God's] love; the surrender of will to [God's] purpose" (Temple, 67). This is a good description of spiritual direction, where we learn not only to "speak the truth" but also to "do the truth."

Theology needs spirituality, just as spirituality needs theology. Spirituality grounds theology in our human experience of waiting and speechlessness and where we are confronted by mystery and our unknowing. Thinking theologically is about learning to speak the truth, which involves a quality of being present to the self-communicating engagement of God with the realities of life. Without this involvement, theology drifts into abstraction and theorizing. Spirituality, when cut off from the truth theology seeks, risks becoming uncritical and self-centered. In this sense, spirituality with its emphasis on practicing the truth, keeps theology tethered to its proper vocation and prevents it from evading its real objective.

Spirituality preserves the disposition and orientation that allows the truth to be recognized and held, yet it is not and should not be limited to interiority. At its best, it always seeks to integrate all aspects of human experience. Reflecting theologically not only opens us up to the truth but also invites us to live that truth and discover that there is never an authentic disclosure of truth that is not also transformative. It is here that spiritual direction is most helpful. We find ourselves learning to express ourselves as truthfully as we can in the presence of another person, and it is the experience of intimacy and vulnerability that we hear ourselves, perhaps for the first time, saying the truth and finding hope, freedom, and the courage to begin to "live the truth."

All this raises the question of "what is true?" In many ways, we distrust our subjectivity, reducing it to a private zone of feelings and intuition. By identifying objectivity with tangible things "out there," the real is often equated with what is visible, and the invisible (including God, the Divine, Spirit) becomes unbelievable. The paradox is true, though—genuine objectivity is the fruit of authentic subjectivity.

We arrive at truth and freedom through being authentic and faithful to our inherent capacity for self-transcendence. Canadian Catholic theologian Bernard Lonergan offers what he calls "transcendental precepts." In this business called life, and in our relationship with the wholly Other, we need to *pay attention* to our experience of reality, *listen to our questions* where we seek to understand what we experience, be alert and *reasonable* as we attempt to discern what is really true, take *responsibility* for ourselves and our world in making decisions in line with that truth, and be *ready for love, to be in love*, and to be in love with love—the love that is in love with us and is our fundamental truth. Authentic subjectivity then points towards another way of knowing and learning and calls us out of our little ego-fixated self into the truth, not only of who we are but also the truth of who God is (Gallagher commenting on Bernard Lonergan, 316).

The theological truths we speak are not ends in themselves; they are evocative rather than explanatory, and whatever they might communicate to us, mere communication is not the goal. The goal is communion. Theological truth is not about an "outside" kind of truth, which is a necessary truth that has to do with facts and analysis. The "inside" kind of truth is the kind of truth that allows me not only to say, "I believe" but also "I am." This truth is not expressed in functional or strategic language but rather in the language of intimacy and mutuality. God wants to wake us up to a quite radical encounter that is participatory, revelatory, and transformative, leading to a realization that God is actually the true subject of our being. Our knowledge of God is always going to be relational; it will therefore be experienced from the inside out. God, "closer to us than our breathing," as Augustine said, is the ground of our being, the Beyond in our midst.

Theological Reflection

Theological reflection has flourished over the past forty years. It is a process where we reflect on our personal or collective experiences in the light of our faith. We all have an innate capacity to reflect, and it is this capacity that enables us to recognize a reality greater than ourselves. In it, we aim to come to a new understanding about the circumstances of our lives and the faith we profess and to identify new ways of responding that reflect our faith and where our actions reflect our truth. Theological reflection is essential to faith, ministry formation, and spiritual discernment. Reflecting theologically asks us to attend to the circumstances of our life, what C. S. Lewis called "interruptions", for he saw that the interruptions are precisely our real life, the life "God is sending us day by day" (Wilson, 188).

While there are many models of theological reflection, all have certain elements in common. Our life experience is crucial, including events we participate in or observe, as are our responses or reactions to those circumstances. Our reflection on life takes place through different lenses: faith tradition, scripture, liturgy, doctrine, reason, community and culture with its often-conflicting voices, values, practices, and perhaps our most basic lens, which involves our own unique life stories. Such reflection serves to bring to our attention what is already present but often deeply hidden. At best, we bring our desire for both authenticity and integrity so we can be open to a new reality—one that is stripped of prejudice and illusion, which makes us vulnerable to change in our feelings, attitudes, and perceptions.

The great Protestant theologian Karl Barth wrote, "Theology is like attempting to paint a bird in flight—not that it is impossible or undesirable, but if we attempt to capture the complexity of the living God by what we know to be the limitations of the human experience, we should not expect to arrive at any immutable rules or revelations" (O'Leary, 122). Theological reflection recognizes, and is a human attempt to express, the impression the "happening" of God has made in and upon our lives. In that "happening," if we believe a communication is made, we listen, pay attention, identify, and discern God's presence, which encourages our response and informs our actions. Through this process, prayer and reflection are enabled, and theology and life—head, heart, and hands come together. Its aim is not an abstraction but rather a human and lived engagement in what Paul VI calls the "dialogue of salvation" (Paul VI, Section 38), which God initiates and leads both to transformation and communion. Theology reminds spirituality that interpretation is intrinsic to experience.

The person who practices theology is not merely using theological tools; he is a theological person. This application of theology is more than an intellectual exercise. It inevitably involves what we now call "contemplation," the action Alan Ecclestone describes as "selfless attention, un-wearying patience, passionate commitment, honesty of purpose, and hunger for truth" (Ecclestone, *Scaffolding*, 2). Reflecting theologically is always self-implicating. Just as the great spiritual classics had as their central question "What or who is God?" so today's question is more likely to be "Who am I?" The two questions are linked. Thomas Merton, in his extraordinary spiritual pilgrimage, with many moments of bewilderment, saw beyond the words he often used, realizing that "what matters in our life is not abstract ideals but profound love and surrender to the concrete judgements of God" (John, 35).

Such attentiveness and personal presence, informed by a persistent and constant submission to the vision of God in the Scriptures and the Christian tradition, suggests, as Rowan Williams says, that "doctrine is a set of instructions for performance" (John, 36), that theology is and must be concerned with action as well as ideas. It involves, by its very contemplative nature, a quality of presence to the reality we reflect upon. It engages the whole person: it is self-involving and self-implicating. It is above all a willingness to be confronted with a truth that will always have the capacity to change us. Theology is therefore not about more information about God as such but rather an actual sharing in God, in God's life, in God's self-knowledge. This will mean learning to see as God sees, and by noticing the unnoticed. The paradox is that our knowledge is a kind of "unknowing," a poverty that speaks less of God (for we are rendered speechless) and one that enables God to speak to us. This is why Paul could say that I will know nothing among you other than Jesus crucified: "always carrying in the body the death of Jesus" (2 Cor 4:12).

The human person fulfills her vocation when she begins to look clearly and live freely in our world. We live work and pray, not in a vacuum but in this broken and fallen world order. Reflection always has a context: and our context is that of multinational corporations, the arms race, the strong state, the economic crisis, urban decay, violence, growing racism and terrorism, the ecological crisis, human loneliness, and the constant struggle between the self and the other. Our invitation is to live in this world without being caught up in its web of wounds and needs, deceits, and illusions. Nothing human is alien to us, and "the roots of all conflict, war, injustice, cruelty, hatred, jealousy, and envy are deeply anchored in our heart" (Nouwen, 34).

We could claim that we simply don't know, but the reality is that deep within us, we don't want to know or face the fact that we all have something to do with the cruelty and envy of this crucified world. We cannot ignore this context and our part in it. Our reflection and prayer must be a daily attempt to "redraw the picture, correcting the distortions, perceiving new immensities, making sharper and clearer what is becoming obscured" (Ecclestone, *Staircase*, 65). The precious gift of spiritual direction offers us a place where we can be heard and a sacred space where we can be seen—as we are—and discover the grace and the freedom of being able to say, "I am." Only then can we become the change we want to see in the world, as Gandhi saw so clearly.

The Difference between the Map and the Journey

There was once an explorer of the Amazon, who, after his amazing trip, went back to his village, where the villagers pestered him to tell them all about his experiences. But he soon found that words could not possibly describe his journey, with all its breathtaking beauty and incredible dangers. So, he suggested drawing a map so that they could go and experience what he did. He drew the map, gave it to them after he had finished it, and they immediately copied the map so that every villager had a copy. After many weeks poring over the map, the villagers themselves became "experts" on the Amazon! The only problem was that not one of them ever went and explored it!

The doctrine or the statements we make about God are not the reality. They are simply signposts to mystery, not ends in themselves. They are "entry points" into the mysteries of faith, not exhaustive descriptions of meaning. The metaphor for this in Buddhist traditions is a teacher pointing a finger at the moon—for a person to really see the moon, the teacher and his finger must disappear. The doctrine points towards an experience, to lived human experience—just as a map could point to a journey. Anything we say about God arises out of lived human experience and speaks into it at the same time.

Doctrines are the result of men and women reflecting on their human experience. The experience comes first, and the function of theological formulation is not to clear everything up, or answer all our questions, but to keep the questions alive and open for further exploration and living as well as the possibility of a genuine encounter with God. The doctrine's chief aim is to encourage us to touch base with our reality, to enter our Amazon. If we try in our theology to answer all the questions, we will miss its proper object, which is to offer us the possibility of a genuine encounter with God. Truth is a mystery to be reverently searched for: it is not and can never be a possession to be jealously guarded and enforced. We are not trying to assimilate the mystery to our mode of understanding: we are always opening ourselves up to the encounter that will mean an inner transformation of the Spirit.

Religious Experience

Liberation theologian Jon Sobrino says, "It is not enough merely to speak of God. Theology must allow God to speak. Theology must move [us] to speak with God. Theology must relate the human being with God" (Sobrino, 71). It must seek to let God be God. We must always be aware of our tendency and need to manipulate or control God for our own ends. We need to be attentive, reasonable, and responsible. Some people hold the view that what we happen to apprehend directly with our five senses is all the reality there is: but as has often been said: *there must be more than this*. This surely is the bedrock of all religious faith. English playwright and TV presenter Dennis Potter wrote: "I see God in us and with us, as some shreds and particles and rumours, some knowledge that we have, some feeling why we sing and dance and act, why we paint, why we love, why we make art" (Potter, 5–6).

Shreds and particles and hints and guesses: this is the way it is for us with our God. As Welsh Anglican priest-poet R. S. Thomas said, "This is our condition. We are always about to comprehend God, but inasmuch we are creatures and finite, we will never succeed.... But by trying to seek it, by longing for it ... we will succeed in maintaining its possibility" (Thomas, *Selected Prose*, 164). He went on to say, in a radio interview with Lord Harries: "I have found a hare's form on the hillside, and I have been able to put my hand in it and feel it still warm, and this is my feeling of God- that we don't actually find him, but we find where he has been."

Humanity needs "this sense of beyond-ness in the midst of the whole of life to revive the springs of wonder and adoration" (Taylor, *Go-Between God*, 45). Such moments like these gift us: they contain within them "promise," arousing within us longings and desire: they are like, as C. S. Lewis says, the "scent of a flower we have not found, the echo of a tune we have not heard, scenes from a country we have not visited" (Wilson, 207). This is not dissimilar to Jesus's words: "The wind blows where it chooses, and you hear the sound of it, but you do not know where it comes from or where it goes" (Jn. 3:8).

All our experiences of God are indirect, mediated through our experience of creation, and this enables us to see what all the time was there but what we have so often failed to acknowledge. "Surely the Lord is in this place, and I did not know it," exclaimed Jacob, waking from a dream. According to Dermot A. Lane, "We do not project, create or posit God in experience. Rather we find God, already there ahead of us in experience" (Lane, viii). Eugene Peterson said, "The assumption of spirituality is that always God is doing something before I know it. So, our task is not to get God to do something I think needs to be done, but to become aware of what God is doing so that I can respond to it and participate and take delight in it" (Peterson, 4). Our goal is not enlightenment but wholeness, a gathering of all the fragments: "an acceptance of this complicated and muddled bundle of experiences as a possible theatre of God's creative works" (R. Williams, 2). Whatever is happening to us, our everyday experience—good, bad, or indifferent—this is sole place where God is disclosed. The sacred is to be discovered in what moves and touches us, in the ordinary rather than the extraordinary, in the "warmth and sweetness and dryness and terror of actual living" (H. A. Williams, 24).

While God meets us and addresses us in the ordinary and the real, it is an encounter that is neither instantly accessible nor easy to identify or articulate. The stark reality is that this experience cannot be contained in words, images, or definition; in fact, it cannot even be contained in our experience. There is, if you like, a "surplus of meaning" in every experience: "God is a beckoning word," says Gerald W. Hughes, beckoning us in and through and beyond all that we ever experience into a place of possibility, promise and mystery" (Hughes, 31).

The first and last word that we can have about the Divine is that we do not know him. Whatever we say of God, and whatever images of God we may use, hides God more than reveals him. The tradition is clear: "If you know God, it is not God!" "God lives in inaccessible light, whom no-one has seen, and no-one is able to see" (1 Tm; 6:16). Meister Eckhart even went so far as to say that the praying person must become "godless" to experience God, for "God is beyond God...I pray God, that He may rid me of God" (Smith, 40). God is simply beyond images and definitions. This is a final eclipse of anything we might say about God, an eclipse even of our comprehension of God.

How We Know God

Jesus speaks to us out of his lived experience of God—his inner experience of the reality of God. And he wants us to grow in our experience and understanding of God. Jesus wants to move us away from an object-subject relationship with God: he wants us to move away from thinking God is "out there," as if God is but one of many objects. As Rowan Williams says: "Knowledge of God is not a subject's conceptual grasp of an object, it's sharing what God is" (R. Williams, 13). Olivier Clément says, "God is not exterior evidence, but the secret call within us" (Ware, 18). All knowledge of God is a sharing and a mutuality, and such knowledge is always participatory. As R. S. Thomas has written:

> *for one like me*
> *God will never be plain and*
> *out there, but dark rather and*
> *inexplicable, as though he were in here.*

—Thomas (*Collected Poems*, 364)

Such knowledge of God is the heart's knowledge, the knowledge that is born of love. The fourteenth century anonymously written *Cloud of Unknowing* says, "God can be taken and held by love but not by thought" (Walsh, 130). This is not to say that thinking and loving are opposed: our thinking and questioning are essential and are to be in the service of loving. Evelyn Underhill, when she edited *The Cloud* in 1912, said in her introduction that its author was both "a deep thinker as well as a great lover" (Taylor, *Christlike*, 3). This is why living and acting contemplatively is so important as we discern through all the complexities of life the movement, activity, and invitation of God. We might say that God is copresent in everything that happens. So we could say that in experiencing God, we experience God not as something seen in the world but rather as the basis of all our seeing, not as an object we know but rather as the basis of all our knowing, not as a thing of value but rather as the ground of all our valuing, the source of all beings and the ultimate context in which all things and meanings subsist (Gilkey, 296).

The inter-connection between theology and spirituality is crucial in the ministry of spiritual direction. If we fail to consider the significance of theology for the spiritual life, we lose sight of the ultimate purpose and goal of life itself. Theology's ultimate goal, and the spirituality and the practical ministry of spiritual direction it serves, is always about seeking and finding the truth, living it, and letting its truth shape us, form us, and keep us. The questions "Who is God for me?" and "Who am I?" are the constant focal points in the spiritual direction conversation, and they can only be resolved in the self-implicating question "Whose am I?"

John V. Taylor, in *The Primal Vision*, a book about Christian presence amid African religion, said that Africans believe that presence is the debt they owe to one another. This primal vision is of a world of presences and is at the very heart of the practice of spiritual direction. The spiritual director has nothing to offer unless she "offers to be present, really and totally present, really and totally *in* the present" (Taylor, *Primal*, 63). She understands that love is not only God's meaning but also her meaning and our meaning. This encounter with the living God is the wellspring of her ministry. Her relationship with those who come to her for spiritual direction will be graced, revelatory, and transformative as she experiences life and God in the poverty of "unknowing." Of course, for her, theology is important, but only a theology that is at heart sacramental, grounded in the realities of everyday experience and life, and that acts as an impetus for engagement and "close attention to reality at every moment, and great fidelity to God as He reveals Himself, obscurely, in the mystery of each new situation"

(Merton, *New Seeds*, 32).

For the spiritual director, theology, like poetry, "is not a hiding place. It is a finding place" (Winterson, 40). The focus for spiritual direction will not be around the question of whether this or that doctrine is true: "There are questions we are the solution to" (Thomas, *Collected Poems*, 263) for what God is always asking of us is that we be both real and authentic. Just as we began with Etty Hillesum, who wanted to be the "thinking heart" of the concentration camp, we can affirm that the true vocation of those involved in the ministry of spiritual direction is to become, as Etty was, fully alive and fully human—a "thinking heart"—speaking, doing, and living the truth in such a way that leads us towards the marriage of head, heart, and hands.

PART III

"The self-giving of the incarnation culminates in the resurrection as the beginning of the transformation of reality from within"

—Denis Edwards (87)

CHAPTER EIGHT

"He clothed with our flesh and we invested with his Spirit"[6]: Spiritual Direction and the Wonder of the Incarnation

The incarnate Word is with us,
Is still speaking, is present
Always, yet leaves no sign
But everything that is.

—Wendell Berry (203)

The first photographs of Planet Earth in the late 1960s astounded the world, and Neil Armstrong recalled how, from the moon, he could "block out the entire earth with his thumb." A later astronaut, Russell Schweickart, saw this planet—our home—as a "bright blue and white Christmas tree ornament ... so small and so fragile and such a precious little spot" amidst the "black sky and the infinite universe." And this little spot, Schweickart said, contains "everything that means anything to you. All of history and music and poetry and art and war and death and birth and love, tears, joy, games, all of it on that little spot out there and you can cover with your thumb..." (Schweickart, 16). These astonishing photographs offer us a breathtaking image of our place in the whole of creation, our common history, and our common humanity, as well as the possibility of revisioning ourselves and our world without boundaries, challenging and critiquing our obsession with tribal loyalties and nation states.

---

6 This quote can be found in Anglican Priest Donald Allchin's *The World Is a Wedding: Explorations in Christian Spirituality*, page 36

All these reflections are reminiscent of Julian of Norwich's vision of the hazelnut in the palm of her hand, so small, that she "marveled that it could be, for [she] thought it might have crumbled" (Julian, 5). And it was her conviction, forged in the crucible of experiencing the "marvelous mixture" of being human, the mixture of "well-being and woe" (Julian, 77), she said, that this tiny nut, so small and yet the ground of all humanity, was held together by love, and that love was not only God's meaning but our meaning as well.

Julian's understanding that "love was his meaning" (Julian, Chapter 86) came about because she was grasped by a vision and an experience of the crucified Christ, enabling her to see our unity with Christ in his human suffering and to center her life on the human image of God and the divine image of humanity. Centuries later, Dietrich Bonhoeffer, the great German theologian killed in the last days of World War II, wrote, "To be a Christian does not mean to be religious in a particular way... [but rather] allowing oneself to be caught up in the way of Christ" and to participate "in the suffering of God in the life of the world" (Bonhoeffer, 123). This has profound implications for the ministry of spiritual direction, for Jesus came, not to offer us a message so much as the possibility of an encounter, and not to offer us a particular way of being religious, but rather a universal way of being human. In British American poet W. H. Auden's *For the Time Being: A Christmas Oratorio*, we can follow the star to the nativity crib and, in the encounter with the humanity of Jesus, discover and value the gift of our own humanity.

> *To discover how to be human now*
> *Is the reason we follow this star*
>
> —W. H. Auden (28)

Our vocation, as human beings, is just what Irenaeus saw in the second century, that "the glory of God is a human being fully alive"

(Clément, 265). This evokes the patient nurturing of the heart and mind, such that we are open to reality, with all its difficulties and questions, its joys, and griefs. Life, the context and focus for spiritual direction, asks of us an unabashed passion for the truth. If God is going to be real to us, then we must in our own way be as real as possible ourselves.

Spiritual direction is both encouraging and respectful as well as confrontational and challenging. This means that we cannot hide from or evade the difficult issues. In our wounded and wounding world, we must face our propensity for illusion and lies, our projections of fear and anger onto others, and our willingness to settle for second best. Such a disposition enables us to move from a life of striving, achieving, and competing, entering more fully into a stance of "wholly attending," not only to the negative and difficult things that all of us face but also alive to the secret impulse for life and love that is our hidden, waiting-to-be-explored treasure.

What seems so decisive and authoritative was the way Jesus embodied the very dispositions he spoke of and seemed to resonate so strongly with the people of his day. The crucial element of his teaching, and especially his presence, was that he appeared as one who dared to assume a unique, intimate, personal closeness with God, whom he called Father. The incarnation, far from being simply an event of the past, opens up for us the possibility of participating in the inner experience of Jesus. So, the Jesus event, the Word made flesh, is an event of the present as well as the past, a taking of our flesh into God and the breathing of God's Spirit into humanity.

The Holy Spirit comes as a gift, offering us not a dogmatic abstraction of a doctrinal statement "out there" but rather an encounter with a truth lived from the inside—God's truth—which we experience as the very truth of our own existence. John Robinson suggests, "The mystery of the Christ is primarily a matter of *recognition*—not, Can you believe this individual to be the Son of God? but rather, Can you see the truth of your humanity given its definition and vindication in him?" (Robinson, 16). In other words, the real question is not whether this or that doctrine is true but *Am I true?* We might say the doctrine of the incarnation is the extreme paradox, an unfathomable mystery, but in the words of former archbishop of Canterbury Rowan Williams, it is nevertheless "a set of instructions for performance" (Williams, 36), which can serve as freeing and transforming our understanding about belief and spiritual direction. Williams offers a wonderful example of a possible dialogue between spiritual director and directee:

> *Tell me about God.*
> *Watch.*
> *What does the doctrine of the Trinity mean?*
> *Watch.*
> *Why should I confess Jesus as Lord?*
> *Watch.*

—Williams (36)

Watchfulness, as the Desert Fathers saw so clearly, was the key to realizing that "there are questions we are the solution to," and far from merely thinking about God, faith, as Anselm saw, is always in search of understanding, an invitation and initiation into an entirely different way of thinking about the divine. Faith, far from mere intellectual or rational conviction, is always about our willingness for commitment and engagement. Put differently, faith is lived out in practical and practiced ways that free us and change us. God cannot be encountered other than in and through created reality, communicating with us in the finite medium of the created earth, just as Judaism understood God as the reality working in and through history. As Saint John says in John 1:18, "No-one has ever seen God directly." All our knowledge and understanding—including our knowledge and understanding of God—is derived from our lived experience of the created world. According to Sam Keen, "The sacred must be rediscovered in what moves and touches us, in what makes us tremble, in what is proximate rather than remote, ordinary rather than extraordinary, native rather than imported" (Keen, 159). What we might call the sacramental imagination opens us up towards a new way of looking and living in the world. This leads us to discern the reality and presence of the Divine in and through the created order, waking us up to the "forgotten blaze of astonishment at our own existence" as G. K. Chesterton says, adding that "the object of the artistic and spiritual life is to dig for this sunrise of wonder" (Chesterton, 94–95).

In some ways, we could say that creation itself is a form of "incarnation," for creation, however obscurely, mediates traces of the divine power and presence, all of which find fruition and fulfillment in the Christ event. We could even say that creation from the beginning is oriented towards incarnation. If God becoming a human being is an act of self-emptying, then the creation itself is an act of self-emptying love—both actions being a renunciation of the exercise of power and freedom. Such an affront to our wisdom and understanding is, at one level, the "foolishness of God," and at a deeper level, the moral imperative that asks of us a response of commitment and loyalty, and the realization that, if we are to be true to ourselves, we are called into a life of self-giving love. Such commitment "carries conviction only to those who are willing to be fools of love, who feel in their heart of hearts that, however far their own performance may fall short, sacrificial love is the highest of all values" (Baker, 405).

As we reflect on the incarnation, we must not minimize its redemptive character, as it has its origins in the creation, so it looks forward in a hidden and deeply mysterious way to the resurrection and the promise of the restoration of all things. Humans experience themselves as people seeking and searching for something more. Not just meaning or purpose but also a sense of permanence and personal enlargement. As Saint Augustine famously said, "Our hearts are restless until they find their rest in God" (Augustine, 1). From this perspective, the resurrection can be seen as a kind of horizon, the realization of our deepest aspirations. Then, it is not some event external to humankind but rather the fulfillment of a sacred truth inherent within the heart of every human life, where we hope for joy through sorrow as well as meaning through absurdity and tragedy. Though as Hannah Arendt said, we "must die, we are born in order to begin" (Arendt, 222). And striking at the same feeling, Simone Weil wrote, "At the bottom of every human being, from the earliest infancy until the tomb, there is something that goes on indomitably expecting, in the teeth of all experience of crimes committed, suffered and witnessed, that good and not evil will be done to him. It is this above all that is sacred in every human being" (Jones, *Pilgrimage*, 45).

Spiritual companioning, or spiritual direction, is a time-honored way of helping one another into this dispositional approach to life. Such companioning becomes a source of encouragement—a welcoming, receptive, and respectful space where we discover the secret, hidden beauty and wonderful potential of what it is to be a human being. Sandra Schneiders testifies that the "basic disposition [openness of heart, the basic readiness to see and hear what is really there] to accept the truth is what enables the person, regardless of moral weakness and lapse, regardless of ethnic or religious background, regardless of orthodoxy, regardless of religious education or lack thereof, to be interiorly 'taught by God' (John, 6:44-45). Such a person, no matter how far astray he or she might have wandered, remains tractable and can be drawn by the Father to Jesus" (Schneiders, 88).

Helping others to express themselves and to be comfortable when words cease encourages them to see beyond the anxieties that so often surround belief. Seeing beyond the shame of things done or not done, and beyond the fear that "I am not good enough, religious enough, or loving enough," is one of the great gifts spiritual direction and companionship can offer. Dag Hammarskjöld wrote in his journal that "the best and most wonderful thing that can happen to you is that you should be silent and let God work and speak" (Hammarskjöld, 134). The God who is known in and through the incarnation in the power of the Holy Spirit incarnates God-self in our lives through the same Spirit. It is the gift of spiritual direction to awaken us to the reality of living in the truth of what Christ's incarnation promised.

Far from being a theological idea of something that happened "back then," this points to a transformational experience and encounter that enable us to "practice resurrection" rather than simply believe it and participate in it as a way of life.

In the second part of this chapter, we will look at six areas of our human life through the lens of the incarnation and see just how these aspects of our lived experience provide fruitful starting points for the ministry of spiritual direction. Each section ends with a few questions that alert us to the living Word that is continually inviting us, through focused and practiced habits of heart and mind, into life. These six areas are:

- The mystery of God, ourselves, and life itself
- As human beings we do not have bodies, but are our bodies
- Our identity is a given and expressed in being able to say "I am"
- We become persons through our relationship with God and each other
- We are incomplete, and as human becomings, we yearn for fulfillment
- Accepting and surrendering our poverty in love is our treasure

"Mysteries must/Be our way of life"
—Elizabeth Jennings (183)

Spiritual direction is a place of welcome, where a spiritual directee is offered the space and the encouragement to pay attention and focus on what they are experiencing. As they begin to express themself, the spiritual director will be alert to the need to create an environment—a kind of "holding pattern"—where the directee will, in time, be able to step back a little, pause, and hopefully find a larger context for their experience, and in that, find new meaning. Spiritual direction values listening, waiting, and hesitation, always seeking to create a space by drawing back and allowing through humble hospitality, so that the other may attend to and give voice to, their experience. For everything we experience in this world is a kind of parable, disclosing and concealing at the same time its hidden and deeper meaning. For the world has depth and richness, beckoning us to marvel at what Denise Levertov described as:

> *the mystery*
> *that there is anything, anything at all,*
> *let alone cosmos, joy, memory, everything*
> *rather than void*

—Levertov (192)

Yet so often we want to reduce mystery to rational clarity. But we are enfolded in mystery. We are a mystery to ourselves—and God, who is both divine and human in the person of Jesus, remains beyond our rational comprehension. "But instead of assimilating this mystery [of God] to our mode of understanding," as Orthodox theologian Vladimir Lossky says, "we should, on the contrary, look for a profound change, an inner transformation of spirit" (Lossky, 8).

This is why the spiritual director hesitates. She steps back and relinquishes her own opinions, projections, and interpretations, offering, as a good host does, the space within which God can act. Through such self-effacing listening, the spiritual directee may begin to hear an invitation into a deeper engagement, into his heart, for as *The Cloud of Unknowing* famously articulated, "[God] can be taken and held by love but not by thought" (Walsh, 130). Mysteries invite reflection and questioning, but ultimately, they are to be lived and embraced, offering us an involved, committed, and imaginative way of being in the world.

The poet John Keats offers us a way of living with all that is unresolved in our life and beliefs. He called this disposition "*Negative Capability* ... that is, when a man [*sic*] is capable of being in uncertainties, mysteries, doubts, without any irritable reaching after fact and reason" (Enright and de Chickera, 257). The spiritual director can help us to become aware of the twin dangers of being too certain, missing the gift that is on offer, and self-assurance, where we simply rely on our limited experiences and perspectives. What the spiritual director offers is space, silence, and time where both the human experience of the directee, with all its issues and contradictions, fears and doubts, *and* the divine reality, can belong together in a fruitful relationship.

As you think about your life and your present experience, what is it that stands out? Can you name your fears or anxieties or what you worry about? Are you fostering habits of the heart that offer a sense of space, solitude, and silence? Is that helpful, or does it cause further anxiety or restlessness? If and when you sit still, are you able to find a certain acceptance of your failings and inability to understand fully, yet at the same time acknowledge and live out of a transforming sense of self in the presence of the mystery of love? Are you willing and able to let go of certainty in matters of faith and staying attentive, reasonable, and responsible, allowing yourself to discover authentic life through self-emptying and being-in-love? What place do you have in your life for relaxation, for music and the arts, and the enjoyment of nature?

"The body is the spirit incognito."
—Sandor McNab (Keen, i)

Again, the real miracle of Jesus of Nazareth was the way he was with people. Beyond words, it was his capacity to reveal himself as genuinely present, standing still in their presence, looking at them, and eliciting from them their often-hidden needs or desires that was truly miraculous. Such presence reveals itself in simple gestures: a smile, a look, the tone of voice. Such presence is embodied and is at the heart of spiritual direction, and it suggests that being seen and recognized is one of the most basic of human needs. As Thomas Merton says, this "deepest level of communication is not communication, but communion. It is beyond words" (Merton, *Contemplative*, 308).

Presence means being available, exposing ourselves to the other. In such a graced interpersonal encounter, our every thought, word, and action are touched and shaped. This is what we mean by intimacy, where, as Robert Dessaix proclaims, "we experience a transparency, where we are softly penetrated to every corner by another's knowing gaze" (Dessaix, 254). Present means both "gift" and "now," and spiritual direction reminds us that we do not need to alienate the spiritual from the material, nor do we need to be defensive and overly protective but rather open and vulnerable, alive to our erotic connection with everything that is. Becoming more fully human and alive will always mean coming home to our bodies, being ourselves, valuing our sexuality, and learning, as Mary Oliver said, "to let the soft animal of your body love what it loves" (Oliver, 14). As Tertullian said, "The flesh is the hinge of salvation" (Casey, 13), and Julian of Norwich similarly affirmed that "God is in our sensuality" (Julian, 55). It is not that we have bodies, we *are* bodies, and if we try to escape this reality, we end up denying ourselves.

My body is my bridge to the world and to other people. Identifying with my body means I can no longer fantasize or live in an illusion. Things happen to my body, which means that my very essence is involved in something over which I have no ultimate control. There is always something more, however. The world has depth, a horizon that is ultimately and mysteriously unknowable, yet is as important as the limited knowledge I have of my finite world. The spiritual director's presence enables the directee to embrace his world as the only place where his life exists and realize that he is inextricably involved in an ultimate and universal mystery that is the very foundation of all that is, sustaining and giving purpose to the known world. In this sense, every person is a frontier where earth stops and heaven begins, the very place of genuine encounter with God. Spiritual direction helps us explore ways to reawaken our sensitivity, awe, and reverence for the things of this world and for the body, its rhythms, grace, and wisdom. The Word became flesh and continues to become flesh.

How care-full and attentive are you to your body? Do you listen to your body, to its needs and its complaints? Or is it a bit of a nuisance? Can you see that our bodies are a bridge to our world, and to others, and at the same time a bridge to God? Is "being a body," rather than "having a body," helpful in moving beyond simply "thinking" about things, often obsessively, and finding more appropriate, creative, and practical ways of action that make a difference? In what ways do you value your sexuality? When you hear the phrase "The Word made flesh," does it confront you with the real human reality of the body of Jesus? Does it confront you with the reality that your body is the place of incarnation? Is there anything that you could do today that would honor your body so that it becomes the very place of encounter with God?

"I am beginning to understand the gospel at the very level of my identity"
—(Ungunmerr-Baumann, 9-11)

Indigenous First Nation elder, artist, and writer Miriam Rose Ungunmerr-Baumann offers this beautiful phrase, which can be seen as a description of the relationship in spiritual direction where the directee begins to realize that his vocation is to discover his true identity, together with his potential, purpose, and capacity to make life-enhancing decisions (Ungunmerr-Baumann, 9-11). This will encompass all the memories, experiences, relationships, and values that make up his sense of self. Living authentically suggests that our identity is both given and discovered and is dependent not in contrast to the other but rather on inclusion, where, as Amin Maalouf comments, we see identity as "the sum of all our allegiances, and within it, allegiance to the human community itself" (Maalouf, 84). This can become, with care, sensitivity, and acceptance, pivotal in a renewed celebration of what it means to be part of the human community. One of the central focal points for spiritual direction will be the fostering of such an inclusive and authentic sense of identity.

The spiritual director's fundamental gift to the other is her own personal vocation to call herself beloved, and this enables her to be available and to receive the other, to assist him in growing more fully into his own potential. As was discussed in chapter two, W. H. Vanstone's helpful insight that to understand someone is to "stand under" them, suggests a certain posture. "It is not the posture of probing into or analyzing, nor is it the posture of grasping, comprehending and mastery," rather, Vanstone explains that one who understands us is "attentive to us and open to receive whatever it may be that we wish to tell or disclose or share" (Vanstone, *Fare Well*, 27). When we understand someone, we are celebrating the fact that God's first gift to us is for us to be able to say, "I am." Hidden even from ourselves, we encounter God, only when we recognize and let go of the self we have both created and believe to be our "real self," surrendering to the process of decentering the self and a coming-to-be centered in an altogether new way in Jesus's own relationship with God. With Saint Paul in Gal 2:20, we can say, "It is no longer I who live, but it is Christ who lives in me," celebrating the wonder of being fully alive and fully human. The spiritual direction relationship has this dual focus—images of God and images of one's self. When Saint Paul spoke of the incarnate Jesus, he often used the phrase "The grace of our Lord Jesus Christ." The Greek word *charis*, for the English word *grace*, is a two-way street, both gift and gratitude and gift and response. For the astonishing revelation in Jesus is that he is both God's "yes" to us *and* our "yes" in response. The spiritual direction relationship is always offered in the breathtaking context of this truth.

When you hear the question "Who am I?" what happens in you? Have you a sense of the givenness and the giftedness of your true self? Or are you still striving to "be" someone or "do" something that will make a difference? When it is mentioned to you that we are often victims of a mistaken identity, that the self we imagine ourselves to be—that busy little preoccupied self with all its goals, desires, fears, and issues—is never remotely the whole of who I am, what happens in you? Can you see how often you seek fulfillment at this level and miss out on the larger life Jesus promises? Beneath this "outer" small self, there is a much more authentic self who can say fully and freely, "I am."

"I cannot be me without you, and we cannot be us without them"
—Alan Jones (195)

A perennial issue for the human being is the haunting question, "Who am I?" There is an even more helpful question, however, moving us to the relational and transformative question, "Whose am I?" Which was precisely Dietrich Bonhoeffer's experience from his prison cell. "Who am I?" he asked...

"Who am I? They mock me, these lonely questions of mine,
Whoever I am, Thou knowest, O God, I am thine."

—Bonhoeffer (173)

The gospels offer us an insight into the relational aspect of Jesus's own identity, and the relationship with a spiritual companion offers us a place where we can experience ourselves as *Imago Dei*, not as individuals, but persons-in-relation. A breakthrough can occur for a spiritual directee when he realizes that his request for spiritual direction is in reality a response to grace, opening him up towards a larger, more expansive God than he might previously have experienced. Rather than defining himself in terms of who he is—a kind of autonomous, self-regulating individual—he has the opportunity in this relationship to begin to explore what it might mean to ask himself, "Whose am I?"

By helping the spiritual directee focus on his relationships—healthy, broken, or nonexistent—the director can help the directee focus his attention outside of himself and towards a transformative vision of his place in the world. Taking someone else seriously is one of the greatest gifts we can offer another that opens us up to a radical shift in awareness to see, perhaps for the first time, how, as Vanstone says, God in Jesus is "totally expended in precarious endeavour" the sake of humanity and all of creation (Vanstone, *Love's Endeavour*, 74). Here in human form is the absoluteness of unconditional love, a love that always makes room for the other and always acknowledges and enriches the other's identity. By her honest receptivity, the spiritual director's prayer is that she will reflect that same unconditional love and receptivity. In a spirit of self-offering and self-emptying, she invites the other into her world and space but always on the directee's terms.

Because of the real need for freedom in every human relationship, the spiritual director offers the directee both hospitality and sensitive confrontation. Other people, as I too often have thought, are not rivals or obstacles to my being "me"; in fact, they are gifts, enabling me to overcome my potential for self-centeredness and self-absorption. "Open arms," a phrase from Miroslav Volf, is a marvelous image for the spiritual director, for open arms signify that I have, as Volf says, "created space in myself for the other to come in and that I have made a movement out of myself so as to enter the space created by the other" (Volf, 141-44). Helping the spiritual directee see that his relationships, however blessed or difficult they are for him, are *the* human problem, the struggle at the heart of all our issues. The other is the place of encounter with the Divine, with the ultimate Other. Spiritual direction helps us to see that following Jesus is to live out, not only the truth of Jesus's existence but also our very own truth. The relationship in spiritual direction is between two human beings in the presence of God. It is as if they celebrate and delight in their humanity in the very sharing of their experience and reflect the human being's innate capacity for empathy and to be "at one" with the other and with God.

How important are relationships to you? Would you say you have healthy relationships with family and friends? Or do they, at least some of them, cause you frustration or anxiety? And what about your dealings with strangers and impersonal situations? Do you find yourself getting angry or impatient? Are you ready to blame the "other" and fail to acknowledge your own responsibilities in human relationships? What practices do you have in place to attend to and consider your relationships with others? As you stay in touch with your relationships, is there anything that suggests that you could do things differently?

"I was born a man[woman], and my task is to become a human being"
—Rabbi Abraham Joshua Heschel (6)

Spiritual direction inevitably comes to focus on one of the great paradoxes of the human condition—that we are incomplete. To realize that is both our glory and our pain. Glory, because there is always more, though often painful, due to the acceptance and continual reminder that our destiny lies elsewhere. The incarnate Christ shows us the vulnerability and precariousness of authentic love. It shows us that woundedness can be a means of healing, and what wounds us to the very core of our being is that we are made for such love, not only to receive it but also to give it. Many of our problems arise from trying to hide from what we really are, resisting the yearning for communion that is authentically ours. For we are always reaching beyond ourselves. Our identity is always in the future, unfolding itself in the ways we seek to express ourselves in language and encounter.

As we pay attention to our lived experience and learn to embrace those places of emptiness and loss, we can see them as "events of the Spirit" and invitations to "die" to the little "me" and find the life that is life indeed. Our experience of incompleteness is not only a desire for more but also a sign of an imminent awakening at the core of our being. We may come to spiritual direction with an almost overwhelming sense of disappointment and failed hopes, and it will require courage to embrace this place of seeming failure and begin to see that it is the gateway to our becoming more fully human and alive. Spiritual direction reminds us that the journey is not principally about blame, shame, or guilt but rather about goodness, commonality, solidarity, and the intimate participation in the mystery of love at the heart of all creation.

The stance and attitude of the spiritual director is crucial, helping another see that our emptiness is a form of readiness and potential. Simon Tugwell urges that we "must learn to be ... incomplete ... a space within which God ... can act" (Tugwell, 49-50). Opening to that space allows the spiritual director to carry out their fundamental task, to "remind people of their capacity for the infinite," as Denys Turner articulated (Turner, xi). The breakthrough occurs when we realize that we only see things, not as they are, but as *we* are. The mystery of Christ, and myself, is primarily a matter of recognition and an awakening of a renewed sense of self—not worrying about whether I believe the creeds so much as realizing that the truth of my humanity is given its definition and vindication in God.

What does the term human becomings *suggest to you? Given your history, temperament, and circumstances, does the journey to "become" seem achievable or simply beyond you? What happens in you when it is suggested to you that, while you are incomplete, you have the capacity for the infinite? The central gift Jesus brings is what he called the Kingdom or Reign of God, not a place to go to but rather an attractive and alternative way of approaching life, imaginatively and wholeheartedly. It is as if he is saying to us, "What if? What is it you most deeply want?" What blocks you from realizing your dream? Is it the circumstances you find yourself in, or is it something in yourself? Attending and identifying the habits of heart that you live by is a crucial step in the journey towards the life that is life indeed.*

> **"But there is only one way into the kingdom—**
> **To be found out in our poverty"**
> **—Monica Furlong (62)**

According to Johannes Baptist Metz, "All the great experiences of life—freedom, encounter, love, death—are worked out in the silent turbulence of an impoverished spirit" (Metz, 49). We resist facing such poverty with everything in our power, which is why spiritual direction can be so helpful. With the help of this practice, we can begin to face head-on our illusions, projections, fantasies, and self-deception. Poverty of spirit is nothing less than the mysterious meeting point between heaven and earth, the only gateway available to us to meet the infinite mystery, the ground of being. Honestly facing ourselves, we begin to see that everything that life offers neither truly satisfies nor provides the security we long for. We are all beggars, caught in a restless quandary, facing a stark choice between self-acceptance and self-alienation, embracing our poverty, or becoming slaves to anxiety. The conversation that is spiritual direction can make a difference, for it is a conversation where silence is as important as speaking; questions are more important than answers; creedal statements, certainties, judgments, and achievements give way to exploration and self-acceptance; and a person can discover, in his poverty and vulnerability, God-given potential and giftedness.

We do not need to seek such poverty, it finds us. It is part of the very fabric of life—"the given life, and not the planned" (Berry, 150). It simply waits to be noticed, embraced, and lived. Through the encouragement of the spiritual director, the directee can find the courage, at last, to face his fears and anxieties, to be himself, and to discover poverty as both a blessed and fertile place. Poverty is a wonderful vocation but with an inescapable tension, and it is of course so different from what we suppose is the religious or spiritual life. Poverty strikes at the heart of our dis-ease and our fearful ability to possess, to be powerful, and to seek prestige, the very temptations of Jesus (Mt. 4:1–11). Spiritual direction can be a gentle and healing space where a person can begin to live with his ego differently, where he can face himself as he is, and wake up to the fact that he can indeed let go of his addictive and destructive attitudes and behaviors. And it is love, *agape* love—what the Polish pope, John Paul II, translated as "solidarity"—that offers this healing, expansive space.

The spiritual director leaves behind learned skills, judgments, and opinions for the other's sake and out of her poverty offers the only thing she can, an inner attitude of receptivity and openness. Spiritual direction can bring out this disposition in someone, allowing them to notice a desire to be free, which, if Saint Augustine is right in saying the "desire to pray *is* prayer," then the desire for freedom *is* freedom, too. The spiritual director comes to this ministry with humility and patience where the other is helped to *recognize* a truth that has, in fact, always been his, a truth now commonly possessed and shared. The spiritual director's task is nothing less than what Turner calls an "evincing of memory... [an] eliciting of nostalgia and desire for the Spirit" (Turner, xi). This is indeed the wonder of the incarnation, and, as Thomas Merton put it succinctly, "We are already one.... What we have to be is what we are" (Merton, *Contemplative*, 308).

Richard Rohr suggests that life inevitably leads us to "a place where we can't fix, control, explain or understand." This is the blessed place Jesus called "poverty of spirit," meaning that you are in the right place when you are poor in spirit. What does that feel like? Our natural response is often to say, this cannot be right, for it feels dreadful. So, what is it like to stay in this place with the feelings this calls out from you ... and in time, can you begin to realize that this is a place of grace, the place where an encounter with truth and life and love is possible? As you think about such poverty, can you get in touch and stay with the countless images of vulnerable people in our wounded and wounding world, affirming that what God revealed for us in the wounded Jesus is both intimately and immediately present to ourselves and those for whom we pray?

***

If we believe in the Incarnation of the Son of God
there should be no one on earth
in whom we are not prepared to see,

in mystery,
the presence of Christ.

—Thomas Merton (*Contemplative*, 229)

The world that we saw in those most beautiful photographs from outer space, captured for the very first time in the long history of our evolving universe, is a place of unimaginable depth and richness. Incarnation says to us that there is only one reality, which is the source and substance of all creation, and astonishingly, we are a part of that reality. But because of our culturally conditioned ego, we identify with only a very small part of that reality. But the ministry and gift entrusted to spiritual companions and directors is to wait patiently, with gentleness, respect, and sensitivity, for that "event of spirit," that "moment of grace," where, in the words that are spoken, a primordial word is heard, a word that emerges into visibility, en-fleshed and embodied in the everyday life of the one who is true to his and her inherent capacity for self-transcendence and love (Rahner, 296). Love is indeed God's meaning. Love is indeed our meaning. "The Word is made flesh." and the wonder of that incarnation has its origins in the whole of creation, which together with all of humanity, secretly and hidden, looks towards the promise and restoration of all things. It is this above all that is sacred in every human being, and this truth is the sacred trust committed to every spiritual director.

CHAPTER NINE

Becoming What We Are: Spiritual Direction in the Light of the Transfiguration of Jesus

The transfiguration of Jesus was a unique event, a question of "reality or vision," as poet Edwin Muir put it (Muir, 198-200). Michael Ramsey, a theologian and former archbishop of Canterbury, acknowledged that while it "does not belong to the central core of the Gospel," it nevertheless "stands as a gateway to the saving events of the gospel, and is as a mirror in which the Christian mystery is seen in its unity" (Ramsey, 144). Variously described as a bridge, vantage point, or watershed, it is neither parable nor miracle, but it is pivotal, in that it lies at a midway point in the Synoptic gospels of Mark, Matthew, and Luke—a crucial moment between the Galilean ministry and the road to Jerusalem and the Cross. The three evangelists describe an occasion in which Jesus takes three of his disciples, a kind of "inner cabinet" of Peter, James, and John, up a mountain where his physical appearance changes and the two greatest prophets of Israel's past, Moses and Elijah, appear beside him in conversation. These two are seen as representatives of the long purposive plan of God, which now finds its fulfillment in Jesus. The disciples are variously described as fearful, bewildered, and without comprehension, with Peter proposing to build three tents, to house Jesus, Moses, and Elijah. Each account links this event to the predictions of Jesus concerning his suffering and death, and Luke uniquely conceives the transfiguration within the prayer of Jesus. Each account recalls the baptism of Jesus in the Jordan River with the words "This is my Son," and each sees the incandescent light in Jesus's face or clothing as an anticipatory experience of the glory of the future coming of the Christ.

Historically, the Eastern Church emphasized the transfiguration's significance, seeing Christ's redemptive work in cosmic terms and the

Christian life as a participation in the new creation. In the Western Church, the focus tended to be on the impact of the transfiguration on the disciples themselves, resulting in an emphasis on discipleship. This difference in some ways parallels the Synoptic gospels recounting the transfiguration as an event, whereas in John's gospel, the transfiguration was not recorded as an event at all but rather as something that permeated the whole gospel in a kind of extended meditation on the glory of God in Christ.

Just as the Johannine and Eastern Church's spiritual emphasis contrasts historically with the more moral and practical emphasis of the Western Church, because of the thirst for re-enchantment, today we see a renewed appreciation of the contemplative life, the recovery of experience in theological reflection, theology's growing appreciation of Trinitarian life and the work of the Holy Spirit, as well as a renewed focus on the transfiguration. The transfiguration then becomes a "lens" through which we see and live more fully in a sacramental universe, enabling us to live with hope in the "between times," living with the "double vision" of the radical empowerment of the Spirit of the Risen Christ on the one hand, while living with the reality of our beautiful but broken world on the other hand (Williams, *What is Christianity?*, 29). The conjunction of the transfigured and the transfiguring One, cross and glory, reality and vision, and suffering and hope is the conjunction we find ourselves and the very focus of the ministry of spiritual direction. Becoming what we already are is the breathtaking vision and impetus humanity needs to live responsibly, creatively, and hopefully in this disfigured world.

Approaching

"The glory of God is a living person and the life of humanity is the vision of God."

—Ireneaus (Clement, 265)

"Jesus took with him Peter, James and John"

—Mark 9:2

Central to our understanding of Jesus of Nazareth is that he creates an image for us of God's attitude both towards creation and humanity. Jesus shows himself as God's self-bestowal in love through self-emptying to the universe. Through the symbols of light and radiance in the transfiguration, we catch a glimpse of the power, glory, and transcendence of God. The Scriptures reveal a people who saw God and the world around them in a new way that radically changed them. As witnesses *of* a profound, life-changing experience, their witness *to* the transfiguration has become for us the means by which we, too, can become participants in the unfolding and present experience of the mystery of Love we call God.

As an "event of the Spirit," the transfiguration shines light on our practice of spiritual direction. As was mentioned in the first chapter, celebrated Australian poet Les Murray speaks of occasions "from earliest childhood ... of a strong, sometimes frightening, sometimes deeply necessary current of meaning in things and in people, *a pressure of significance*" (Tacey, 112). He suggests that these moments are rarely alluded to, as if they did not matter. Just as the Bible itself communicates with us at a nondoctrinal level, the story of the transfiguration can also speak directly into our lived human experience.

Through the ministry of spiritual direction, we can, however falteringly or tentatively, begin to get in touch with the everyday events and circumstances of our lives and realize that there must be more than what our five senses apprehend. Such attention to what we might call our "pre-religious" experience then becomes the focus for spiritual direction. Michael Paul Gallagher says, "People are hungry for a different space of self-hearing and self-healing, and when they find it, they spontaneously start looking for God" (Gallagher, 15). Because, according to Ronald Rolheiser, "long before we do anything explicitly religious at all, we have to do something about the fire that burns within us. What we do with that fire ... the disciplines and habits we choose to live by, will either lead to a greater integration or disintegration within our bodies, minds and souls" (Rolheiser, 10–11). Wherever we are in life, we are already on a journey, and spiritual direction offers us the opportunity to become more intentional and more focused. It is as if "God [is] working anonymously and on the inside: the beyond in the midst," as John V. Taylor intimates (Taylor, 5). In this way, we can begin to see that our journey is one of promise and that the choices and decisions we make are either life-giving or life-denying.

As human beings, we are neither self-contained nor autonomous but rather beings-in-relation. Mark tells us that "Jesus took with him Peter, James and John and led them up a high mountain apart, by themselves." Jesus decides to go, and he decides who will go with him. A whole new world opens to the spiritual directee when she realizes that her decision to enter direction was not simply her initiative but rather a response to grace. Far from robbing her of freedom, this deepens and enhances her appreciation of choice and decision-making and will also help her realize just how intertwined her life is with others. Just as the disciples went together up the mountain, in the spiritual direction relationship, it is important to ask in whose company we are travelling. Who are the ones that populate my life? With whom is my life bound? What is the nature of my relationships with family, friends, and society?

The transfiguration takes place on a mountain, where the long, ascetic Jewish and Christian traditions offer solitude, silence, and the possibility of spiritual detachment and perspective. In spiritual direction, a safe space is created, a kind of mountaintop, offering not so much a sudden or exceptional "other-worldly" spiritual experience but rather a place where a word of grace can be heard, and insight can be gained. The spiritual directee can be assured here that faith is not primarily about mental assent to a set of beliefs but rather about his attitude towards life, his disposition of openness, and the realization that the opposite of faith is not doubt but rather the closed mind. Through the presence, availability, affirmation, and even vulnerability of the spiritual director, he can come to hear a new voice that he slowly recognizes as his own, explore a faint dream he has long carried, express righteous anger, embrace acute pain or loss, accept forgiveness, take responsibility for his own life, and affirm in his heart the mystery and goodness of his being. Seeing things differently and expressing, perhaps tentatively, his inner truth, invites him into a place of decision and transformation.

As spiritual directors, we will pray for openness, respect, and hope. We will seek freedom for ourselves, freedom for the one coming to spiritual direction, and freedom for God to be God. We will seek to be fully present, offering the spiritual directee the space she needs. We will endeavor to let go of my opinions, judgments, and thoughts for her sake. We will seek to listen to her into speech and look at her into life. We will try to offer her a way forward without getting in the way. We will not be telling God what God should be doing; instead, we will pray to be more deeply aware of what God is already doing. In spiritual direction we are engaged in the sacred conversation discussed in the first chapter. Australian writer Don Watson says that "when people make speeches, they attempt an embrace. They say to their audience, 'You and me both': we are for all practical purposes the same" (Watson, 139). It is this vulnerable, self-emptying presence of "being with" the other that is the true gift of spiritual direction. The miracle of Jesus is truly his presence with others. His approach towards us offers us the template for both our approach towards our fellows and towards life itself.

Seeing

"The sight of God is the transfiguring of the human person."

—B. F. Westcott (Ramsey, 62)

"They saw his glory"

—Luke 9:32

"We have seen his glory"

—John 1:14

One key to understanding what the transfiguration meant is Byzantine Greek theologian Gregory Palamas' insight that "Christ was transfigured not by receiving something he did not have before, not by being changed into something he previously was not, but as manifesting to his disciples what he really was, opening their eyes and from blind men making them see again" (Lee, 47). The transfiguration was truly a revelatory event, bearing witness that, as John V. Taylor notes, the Spirit "enables us not by making us supernaturally strong but by opening our eyes" (Taylor, 19). Former archbishop of Canterbury Rowan Williams suggests that "one of the tests of actual faith, as opposed to bad religion, is whether it stops you ignoring things" (Williams, *What Is Christianity*, 21). Such faith Williams says is "most fully itself and most fully life-giving when it opens your eyes and uncovers for you a world larger than you thought" (Ibid). Realizing you can't see is the way forward. Seeing is about being real, finding perspective, and learning to value the given-ness of life as a true gift.

Jesus's diagnosis of the human condition is that we do not see that we are blind and that we too easily live with either illusion, misunderstanding, or, worse, deception. The transfiguration of Jesus has its precedents in the Hebrew Testament. The cloud is the "Shekhinah cloud," concealing and revealing the holiness of God and representing both God's closeness and remoteness. It reminds us of the pillar of cloud that led the Israelites out of Egypt, that hovers over the tabernacle, and that journeys and suffers with the people of God. The revelatory aspect of the transfiguration is that creation itself, of which humanity is an integral part, is the true dwelling place for God. The transcendent glory we see in Jesus, however, is not as the world understands glory. For the glory of God is seen in the self-emptying, surrender, humiliation, and poverty of Jesus in the vulnerability of love, revealing who God is and who we are. No wonder it was hard for the disciples to see and to understand; they were both awe-struck and fearful. As such, "double vision" means being "rich toward God," which can only be experienced through "poverty of spirit."

In spiritual direction, the continuing emphasis is necessarily bifocal. We explore images of God, constantly letting go of distorted, inadequate, or life-denying images and realizing that whatever we say about ourselves is another way of speaking about God. Because God is known and experienced in and through our sense and experience of self, believing becomes another way of saying, "I am." As the tradition has long said, our task is to become what we already are. This ability to say "I am" is nothing less than the subjective sense of being both loved and loveable and is a recognition of the objective reality of God's love.

Mary Oliver writes in one of her poems that "Belief isn't always easy" but that she has learned, "If not enough else/To live with my eyes open" (Oliver, 63). The person coming for spiritual direction—and this can be especially true for those with some religious background—may be weighed down with the pressure of needing to conform to some religious belief. It is true that "belief isn't always easy," and this difficulty can even prevent a person from "seeing" clearly. Acknowledging fear, anxiety, or doubt is often the first step towards faith.

To see clearly means to use our eyes—not merely to look with, but to look through. This kind of attention leads to insight or seeing into the heart or depth of the great mystery. This is not simply intellectual cognition; it moves towards "heart-sight," with the attendant intimacy and vulnerability of genuine relational knowledge, a knowing that is a kind of "unknowing." This is an encounter of an "I-Thou" relationship, and it opens up the possibility of "God-sight," seeing as God sees, seeing the marriage between heaven and earth, divinity and humanity, and the collapsing of the objective-subjective distinction. Here, the disciples are afforded a glimpse of the great "I AM," a revelation of God that is both an astonishing and unsettling self-revelation. This can lead to "fore-sight," that unique gift of the transfiguration, opening up for us a vision of God bringing the whole of creation to its final consummation, utterly renewed and transformed (Ryan, 1).

Our world is a kind of parable, covering and uncovering its richness, depth, and meaning. What we need is what John V. Taylor describes as "the recovery of a sense of 'beyond-ness' in the whole of life to revive the springs of wonder and adoration" (Taylor, 45). The Spirit has "emerged into visibility," as Michael Morwood says, and the transfiguration invites us into this sacramental world of grace (Morwood, 85). This way of seeing is "not instant photography of the world," Alan Ecclestone wrote in *The Scaffolding of Spirit: Reflections on the Gospel of Saint John*, "it is something learned by patient education of our sensibility to the engagement of God with the world" (Ecclestone, *Staircase*, 66). The practice of spiritual direction offers the space and the encouragement for us to wake up to this transformational vision; it means the steady, grace-full inculcation of life-changing habits of mind and heart and body, what Ecclestone calls the "selfless attention, un-wearying patience, passionate commitment, honesty of purpose, and hunger for truth" (Ecclestone, *Scaffolding*, 2).

Yet such vision of the glory of God, of creation and humanity, is not straightforward. The disciples have difficulty in seeing and knowing the startling disclosure that Jesus is the universe's "Yes," its loving, self-transcendent offering to God. This is in many ways utterly beyond our knowing, hence the symbol of the cloud. The goal of spiritual direction is to enable a person to wake up to this extraordinary "Yes," that indeed Jesus is the very truth of our existence, and to find the courage to assent to it.

Listening

"The [human being] is the being created as hearer of the Word, and only in responding to the Word rises to his full dignity"

—von Balthasar (18–19)

"Listen to him"

—Mark 9:7

The belief that God speaks and creates us by addressing and calling us into being, with a life-giving word spoken directly into our lived experience, is at the heart of the Christian faith. We have been "conceived in the mind of God as the partner in a dialogue" (von Balthasar, 19). This word is not a thing so much as an event. German theologian Karl Rahner discusses some words as being "primordial words," human words that are at the same time words of eternity. They are "words which spring out of the heart", gifts of God which bridge the temporal with the infinite. (Rahner, 295–96). In Jesus, God says to us, "I give you my word." He is to be trusted. Jesus is the self-expression and self-communication of God to the universe. He is speaking not only out of his historical context but also out of our contemporary context, and his word is a living word, speaking directly and intimately into our lived experience.

The word of scripture and the word sounding in the depths of our hearts can become a place of meeting. Most of us need reminding that the secret place of our heart, so often neglected and forgotten, is already a place of openness, attentiveness, and willingness. This space, which God clears for us, is where we can listen to Jesus and hear ourselves as well, where we can become fully human and fully alive. Here we "find ourselves *addressed*, and addressed we *find* ourselves," as Sarah Bachelard says, in that contemplation is "a practice of becoming still enough, silent enough, open enough to hear the voice of the 'other'" (Bachelard, 36). The spiritual director seeks to find a way to speak "that resonates with the creative word working in the depths" of the other person. It is an active search for a word to speak into what is real in the spiritual directee. Rowan Williams expounded upon Simon Weil's notion that we "hesitate" in our relationships with others, as we "might do on the threshold of some new territory, some unexplored interior" (Williams, *Silence*, 73–74). This can be a genuine place of transformation, where we see the reality of our life within a larger horizon, and where we learn to live out of our original nature and find both hope and meaning. In this space, the spiritual directee may speak candidly about the ambiguity, contradiction, confusion, joy, and grief of her lived experience, and where spiritual direction can flourish.

Matthew and Mark tell us that Moses and Elijah appear next to the transfigured Jesus. They represent the Law and the Prophets and the Hebrew Scriptures. They are talking with Jesus as he stands in glory. Then Luke adds that they "appeared in glory and were speaking of his departure (or exodus), which he was about to accomplish in Jerusalem," a key phrase that draws us back into the pivotal and utterly central experience of liberation for the people of Israel in the Exodus, which not only freed them but also marked them as God's people (Lk. 9:31). Moses and Elijah appear to encourage Jesus in his central mission of confronting systemic injustice and offering a universal way of freedom and hope. In the person and passion of Jesus, the culmination of Israel's long yearning for deliverance and salvation is represented. In each of the Synoptic gospels, the transfiguration event is both preceded and followed by Jesus' passion predictions that "The Son of man is to be betrayed into human hands, and they will kill him, and three days after being killed, he will rise again," and Mark's comment, "But they did not understand what he was saying and were afraid to ask him" (Mark 9:31–32).

Just as these predictions bewilder the disciples, we too need time to accept this confronting truth. For they open for us not only the truth of Jesus but our own truth as well. Learning Jesus, which is one way of understanding Christian spiritual direction, is always self-implicating. Here we not only face the fact that Jesus' death is no unfortunate accident, but that death, the giving up or handing over of oneself, is the very key to the generation of new life. For without death, there is no fullness of life, or as Ilia Delio muses, "death is integral to who God is—self-giving love" (Delio, 77).

The exodus that Jesus makes is truly a new beginning. However distressing, challenging, and frightening his death is for us, it allows us to confront not only our own death but also the death and end of all things—the end of this world as we know it. The depth and finality of death are of the utmost significance, for they put the resurrection of Jesus into the sharpest view. Our future has already appeared and been anticipated by the transfiguration. From this perspective, spiritual direction is simultaneously reality based and oriented towards hope.

The voice from the cloud directs the disciples to the glorious identity of Jesus as God's Beloved Son. The transfiguration asks us to participate in a different way of knowing and points us towards a reality beyond rational comprehension. With its mythic and imaginative dimension, images, metaphors, and symbols, the transfiguration can speak powerfully to the ambiguity and paradox of our everyday lived experience. By responding to the sensitivity and grace of the spiritual director, a spiritual directee can find herself opening up to the great truth and mystery of life. Too easily, in our need to control, define, and pin down, we miss the richness and depth of life itself. When we are encouraged to slow down and get in touch with what is going on for us, when we give words and emotions both the space and time to express themselves, it is as if a window opens, and we can see and hear beyond. The Word speak to us, with all its immediacy and intimacy.

Following

"When Christ calls a person, he bids him come and die."

—Dietrich Bonhoeffer (79)

"If any want to become my followers, let them deny themselves and take up their cross and follow me."

—Matt 16:24

One of the distinctive themes of the transfiguration story is its emphasis on discipleship. The unique gift of the gospels is that they offer us an encounter with the risen Christ. Christianity is not to be reduced to a set of doctrines or propositions or even creeds, and the genius of the gospels is in following him, companioning him, or rather, letting him companion us. God's love is not merely a loving attitude of God towards us, it is literally God himself committed and involved *with* us.

The gospels offer us the possibility of remembering, learning, and experiencing Jesus, but not in terms of a mere backward-looking "discipleship." Rather, the extraordinary gift offered is for us to "become what we are," or as Saint Paul in Galatians 2:20 would have it, "It is no longer I who live, but it is Christ who lives in me." Such following of Jesus will mean for each of us, and especially for the one coming for spiritual direction, finding the courage to take the next step. As Dietrich Bonhoeffer said, "We shall never know what we do not do" (Taylor, 121).

Liberation theologian Segundo Galilea makes clear that there "does not exist a 'spirituality of the cross,' but one of following him—a following that at times will demand the cross of us" (Galilea, 2). The person coming for spiritual direction, like the disciples, is often faced with the daunting prospect of choice, but with encouragement from the spiritual director, she may discover the freedom of exchanging "a living death for a dying life." In this, she can see beyond the transfiguration as an event and more of a process, a gateway, and an invitation into her journey and her mountaintop experiences, as well as her failures and wrong turns, and experience being transformed, as in Corinthians 3:18, "from one degree of glory to another" (2 Cor 3:18). The transfiguration illustrates to us that our future has already appeared. The human person, Jesus shows us, is not only radically open to God but already totally given over to God in self-offering. At the heart of being human is a deep primordial "Yes" to God, which awaits our conscious and free "yes." This is a transformation of the utmost significance. Who we see in the transfigured Jesus is ourselves—participants and coworkers in the transformation of all things. With Saint Paul in Philippians 1:6, we can say, "I am confident of this, that the one who began a good work among us will bring it to completion by the day of Jesus Christ." Or as Julian of Norwich said, "We can never stop wishing or longing until we fully and joyfully possess him" (Julian, 50).

There is still frustration, groaning in labor pains, as we wait redemption, but the glory that is anticipated and incomplete is already our present possession. New Testament scholar N. T. Wright notes that the gospels "say Jesus is raised, therefore God's new creation has begun, and we've got a job to do" (Stewart, 21). The gospel, properly understood, has less to do with theological propositions to believe than the task of following. Faith, which the spiritual director reminds us of continually, is about taking the next step.

This task is not a chore or a duty; Jesus is not asking us to go against our true nature. What he is saying to us, radical and revolutionary as it is, is that we are most fully ourselves when we give ourselves away. Truth and freedom are always open to us, but only when we stop living as self-determining individuals and fulfill our God-given capacity for self-transcendence, entering the communion or community of loving relationships, which is God. As Saint Paul so clearly saw, in Jesus we see the divine empty God's self and accept all the consequences of living in a violent world. The very human Jesus likewise relinquishes all in an act of self-emptying. Jesus, who moves so decisively from action to passion, invites us to enter his "handing over," to become like him, and even more, to let him live in us, as in Colossians 1:27—"Christ in us, the hope of glory." Because of Jesus, we can say that as human beings we are Christologically and Paschally structured.

To overcome our fear and resistance, we must allow ourselves to fall in love and to be loved. The ministry of spiritual direction is a ministry of love, for only love makes sense of T. S. Eliot's "costing not less than everything" (Eliot, 59). Also, Theodore Roethke says, "Love is not love until love's vulnerable" (Roethke, 31). This is not an invitation to achieve anything, let alone be a success at it. It is a time when we are to hold together our own falling and inadequacy *and* our growing vision of God's love. The spiritual director, with great care and sensitivity, companions us through this time. Only this will help us through what Eliot calls "a life-time's death in love,/Ardour and selflessness and self-surrender." It is only then that we can realize the radical truth that Thomas Merton saw, that "Love is the epiphany of God in our poverty" (Finley, 65).

Praying

"Day after day we must endeavour to redraw the picture, correcting the distortions, perceiving new immensities, making sharper and clearer what is being obscured"

—Alan Ecclestone (*Staircase*, 65)

"Jesus ... went up on the mountain to pray"

—Luke 9:28

Prayer, in Luke's account of the transfiguration, is the motive behind Jesus going up the mountain. The glory that is glimpsed in that event reveals how Jesus lived in profound intimacy and immediacy with God, whom he called Father. It was out of this deep and innermost secret, and in the presence of God's coming Kingdom, that his experience of God was "as a power cherishing people and making them free" (Schillebeeckx, 268). Amid the disciples struggling to keep awake, Jesus is both fully awake and aware, fully human, and fully divine. Jesus is on fire with passion for God and the coming of God's reign of justice and nonviolence, and what he offers is that we might share in his same inner experience. In spiritual direction, this vision invites us to wake up to the deepest mystery and truth about God and ourselves, and to learn to inhabit this space of prayer in our daily lives.

Spiritual direction offers the gift of a broader healing and encouraging space, where real prayer is possible and where we can see our life in the greater context of our remembered past, patiently allowing the present moment to speak to us, realizing that our future may shape us even more than our past. This is a foretaste of the heavenly glory, and Michael Ramsey says that our Christian life is to be lived in reference to this glory. With the whole of creation, we resonate with a dynamic impulse towards self-transcendence, and in prayer, we gather up all history and creation, joining in a response of praise, thanksgiving and saying "Yes" to God. With the world transfigured, we newly discover the radiance and beauty of the whole creation, and, in the face of death, we live with hope because of the resurrection, which the transfiguration anticipates. Ramsey continues his reflection, remarking that "There is no despair, for glory is a present possession: there is no contentment, for a far greater glory is the final goal."

Death and the end of the created order are facts, but as Jesus faces the total darkness and abandonment of death and lives, we can also trust that our death, and the end of the world, will be altogether new and God's doing. Neither simply accepting things as they are, nor fleeing from them, we enter that uniquely Christian disposition that the transfiguration invites us to assume. This is, as Michael Ramsey saw, an "attitude rooted in detachment," wherein we exchange all those things that make up our "living death" for the "dying life," which we have caught a glimpse of in Jesus. This is the constant "rhythm of going and coming" Ramsey says we are called to, ascending the mount, and always descending again and again into this disfigured world (Ramsey, 146). One of the most vivid symbols for us is the bitter irony that August 6, the Church's feast day for the transfiguration, was also the date of that most graphic image of disfigurement in our world, the dropping of the atomic bomb on Hiroshima, the first of two bombings of Japan that ended World War II.

The vision of Jesus in glory allows us to move from despair or resignation into a place where our pain is transformed into a fruitful and creative response that is full of power to work for change where it is possible and to live with promise. Our eyes are always being directed towards our present reality in spiritual direction, yet at the same time holding the vision of the crucified and resurrected Jesus—our future who has already appeared. With this "double vision," we are both utterly realistic and hopeful at the same time, engaged with everything that is, praying as Jesus prays, and learning to see as God sees and to love as God loves.

Just as the mountain is for the disciples a "thin place" in the spiritual direction session, it is as if we are with Jesus in a "thin place," hopefully learning that our human heart is also a "thin place," where the boundaries of heaven, earth, body, and spirit almost disappear. The spiritual direction relationship allows us to be with Jesus on the mount, nurturing dispositions and habits of silence, solitude, expectancy, and openness, where we can come to realize that we are indeed caught up in the very force field of Jesus's own sense of belovedness. In this place, with our spiritual director and with Jesus, perhaps tentatively, not quite fully understanding, we catch a glimpse of God's eternal purpose for us. Here we discover in a breathtaking vision, the completion and consummation of the plan. In Christ, in glory, and in the challenge as we descend the mountain, we are leaving behind our spiritual director, and we must appropriate this vision and become who we already are. Just as Thomas Merton says, "In prayer we discover what we already have. You stand where you are, you deepen what you already have, and you realize that you are already there. We already have everything, but we don't know it. Everything has been given to us in Christ. All we need is to experience what we already have" (Finley, 111). We are like the Byzantine monk who says, "Looking back my impression is that for many, many years I was carrying prayer within my heart, but did not know it at the time" (Louf, 22).

Becoming

"To live is to change and to be perfect is to have changed often."

—John Henry Newman (Ecclestone, *Yes*, 18)

"And all of us ... are being transformed into the same image from one degree of glory to another."

—2 Cor 3:18

Jesus the Christ, made of star dust like us and part of the created order, communicates that we are part of the universe now becoming what it was made for—immediacy, intimacy, and union with God in glory, forever. The transfiguration is both an epiphany and a theophany, disclosing and revealing the full identity of Jesus while providing an unmistakable revelation of God, allowing the disciples, and us, to interpret the whole of Jesus's life and death in terms of the full glory of God, considering God's luminous future. This is all done through the symbol of light—what the Eastern Church describes as "uncreated light," the very essence of God's self, a light neither material nor spiritual but transcending entirely the order of creation, apprehended not by sense, yet overwhelming in its intensity and beauty. The very human Jesus on the mountain stands at the threshold of heaven, and as God has shared human nature, offering that humanity may come to share the divine nature. The celebrated formula of the Fathers was that "God became what we are that we might become what he is" (Clement, 263).

"Becoming what we are" is a breathtaking experience for us. The ministry of spiritual direction is always offered as a visionary key opening us up to the possibility of genuine freedom and hope. In and through this ministry, we are invited, in the light of the transfiguration, to value everything that is made. Part of the wonder of being alive is the realization that our existence is the result of an unimaginably long, complex, and finely tuned series of events. Just as the Spirit at the transfiguration illuminates the glorious Christ, the same Spirit also permeates all creation and dwells in every individual creature and the whole community of creation. This same Spirit is intimately involved in the ongoing process of evolution at the most basic level, creating mutual and harmonious interactions, promoting a life of cooperation and community. This is the very vision of Saint Paul, with its emphasis on longing and yearning, the desire of the whole of creation to be redeemed with the children of God (Rom 8:22). Yet this presence of the Spirit in creation is a sign of the self-limitation of God. The Spirit does not dominate, it allows the creation, including every human being, to reach towards God. In the sufferings of the created order, with its evolutionary dead ends and the whole history of human failings, crimes, and catastrophes, the transfiguring Spirit is present, suffering with and longing for the redemption and transformation of all things.

And the stark reality of this mountaintop event is that, despite Peter's wish to build three booths to stay there, the disciples are to come down from the mountain. The journey involves an ascent up the mountain and treasured times of insight and affirmation, but it always thrusts us back into the everyday of our beautiful but broken world. In that descent, Jesus finds the other disciples arguing among themselves, unable to heal a boy possessed. It is at this point where the boy's father makes the touching plea, "I believe, help my unbelief," expressing a faith and a prayer that acknowledges our helplessness, impotence, and our need of grace (Mark 9:24). The transfiguration has disclosed Jesus in his hidden glory, power, and authority, but it is discerned through faith and prayer. This is the "double vision," or as Julian of Norwich calls it, the "marvelous mixture of both weal and woe," that spiritual direction asks us to hold (Julian, Chap. 52). It is the harsh and difficult territory of powerlessness and unbelief, the reality of sin and failure, which is precisely the place where we are to learn the truth and glory of Jesus.

We are all deeply flawed, but to know that we stand on holy ground is the fundamental gift of spiritual direction. The transfiguration invites us to see the hidden mystery of God's love and power amid this wounded and wounding world. Julian of Norwich's experience was that sometimes we are consoled; at other times, however, we are bereft, but "God wishes us to know that he safely protects us in both sorrow and joy equally" (Julian, 15). Such faith and prayer ask us to see beyond the horizons of this world and to look at our world and our experience of it, including the wounds we all share, while seeing the glorious scars of the Risen Christ.

The transfiguration is a miraculous invitation to see the costly love of God, who, in Jesus, is his own response. Julian's great insight was that "our Lord's meaning was love" (Julian, Chap. 86). What Jesus discloses in the transfiguration, what he accomplishes in the Paschal Mystery, is "who" God is—Love. He discloses that our name too is Love, that when God looks at us, God looks with love and at love. We are, from Elizabeth Johnson's experience, "essentially constituted by relation to God, [so] even in the shattering of death one is held in communion by this relation of Love, which always and everywhere creates a new being" (Johnson, 194). Nothing can or will separate us from this Love. Rowan Williams says that "God desires us *as if we were God*, as if we were the unconditional response to God's giving that [God] makes in the life of the Trinity" (Myers, 90). This love is indeed "ecstasy," Pope

Benedict XVI says, an "exodus out of the closed inward-looking self towards its liberation through self-giving, and thus towards authentic self-discovery and indeed the discovery of God" (Benedict, 13). The ministry of spiritual direction, to be faithful to its calling, holds up this vision and invitation—to learn "that God loves us as God loves God." Can we let the transfigured Christ seduce us? Can we let ourselves fall in love with love, the love of a God who pours God's self out in creation and incarnation, anticipates the future through his transfiguration, and sets it in motion through his resurrection?

Centuries apart, there are two witnesses to the overwhelming and empowering vision of the transfigured Christ. From the desert tradition, "Abba Joseph came to Abba Lot and said to him: 'Father, according to my strength I keep a moderate rule of prayer and fasting, quiet and meditation, and as far as I can I control my imagination; what more must I do?' And the old man rose and held his hands towards the sky so that his fingers became like flames of fire and he said: 'If you will, you shall become all flame'" (Ward, xii). And in the twentieth century, Pierre Teilhard de Chardin said, "The day will come when, after harnessing the ether, the winds, the waves, the tides , gravitation, we shall harness for God the energies of Love. And on that day, for the second time in the history of the world, [we] will have discovered fire" (Teilhard de Chardin, 86-87).

***

The transfiguration provides an astonishingly illuminating lens through which to see both the inner dynamic and charism of spiritual direction. It throws light on both the disposition and presence of the spiritual director and the movement and growth in the directee's relationship with the Divine. The holy place of the transfiguration, offered through the ministry of spiritual direction, allows the spiritual directee glimpses of grace in her everyday lived experience and growth in self-awareness and self-confidence in her own sense of belovedness. All this suggests a new intentionality in her approach to life and the desire to exercise the spiritual practices of patience, openness, and attention. A new sense of wonder at the whole of creation, and her own place in it, reorients her towards a life of reverence, gratitude, and responsibility, awakening her to the realization of just how important her choices and decisions are, not only for herself but also for the whole of creation.

The transfiguration affords us the possibility of awakening to God's resounding "yes" to the universe and to humanity. This "yes" is God's self-offering in love through vulnerable self-emptying. At the same time, the transfiguration anticipates and celebrates the passion and resurrection of Jesus, whereby we see that at the heart of being human is a deep primordial "yes" to God, and it is this "yes" that now awaits our conscious and free "yes." This is the promise of the transfiguration and the gift of spiritual direction—that in this disfigured world, our "yes" has already been offered to God. But it is a costly "yes," for death is integral to God, who is self-giving love, and this is our truth too. What we see in Jesus is ourselves—participants and coworkers in the transformation of all things. It is here that we can gather up all of history and creation and join in that response of praise and thanksgiving to God. It is here, in the transfiguration of Jesus, that we see ourselves as part of a universe now becoming what it was made for, namely union with God. Our world as it is, together with our transfigured world, is the true context for spiritual direction.

"There is another world, and it is this one."

Patrick White, the Australian novelist attributed this quote to French poet Paul Éluard and used it as an epigram to his novel The Solid Mandala. *It is this utterly transformative vision of both God and humanity, and the cosmos, that enables us to say we are becoming what we already are.*

CHAPTER TEN

"Let him easter in us"[7]: Spiritual Direction and the Promise of New Life in the Paschal Mystery

Thinking about the resurrection is a bit like looking at a butterfly in the garden: flying, catching the light of the sun, and just out of reach. The moment you catch it in your hand, its beauty, invitational aliveness, and mystery have gone. When it comes to thinking about the resurrection, it is hard for us to let the mystery live and speak its truth. Like the butterfly, we want to grasp it, understand it, even pin it down. But in all our analysis and interpretation, we fail to appreciate that its truth will always be beyond our grasp.

We ask all sorts of questions about the resurrection: "Did it really happen?" and "How did it happen?" But by asking such questions, we fail to realize "there are questions we are the solution to" (Thomas, 263). We keep the resurrection "back there," failing to see that its truth is not what we might call an "outside" kind of truth, a truth that is the conclusion of philosophical or scientific inquiry, but rather a truth profoundly and intimately connected to who we are. We create for ourselves an endless puzzle for our minds, not realizing that as a mystery it is, and will remain, an inexhaustible truth that is out of our reach. This mystery, nevertheless, makes all the difference in how we see our world, ourselves, each other, and God, and how we live our lives.

---

7   This chapter's title comes from "Let him easter in us" in *The Wreck of the Deutschland: Poems and Prose of Gerard Manley Hopkins*. London: Penguin Books, (1953) 1963, p. 24.

What happened "out there" or "back then" and what happens "in here"—for the disciples as much as for us now—are pieces of a whole. Our knowledge of God is not knowledge as the object of our analysis or scrutiny but, paradoxically, knowledge of ourselves, as beings who are utterly dependent on God. Our knowledge of God is participatory, intuitive, subjective, experiential, and relational, more akin to communion than intellectual apprehension. What poet R. S. Thomas says about prayer could be said about the resurrection: "It is the annihilation of difference, / the consciousness of myself in you, / of you in me" (Thomas, 263).

It is not so much an assimilation of the mystery of God to our understanding as entering another way of being and knowing. This mystery interrogates us and invites us into a profound change of heart and an inner transformation of spirit. Our knowledge of God is "a journey, an ongoing exodus out of the closed, inward-looking self towards its liberation though self-giving, and thus towards authentic self-discovery and indeed the discovery of God" (Benedict XVI, 13). This transcending of the self and living the experience of self-giving is just like falling in love and being drawn out of the little self into the larger life of being in communion. No wonder that philosopher Ludwig Wittgenstein could say, "It is love that believes the resurrection" (Bachelard, 52).

The resurrection occurred in the silence of the tomb. In many ways, we can say the resurrection is an event, a happening, an historical event—albeit at an enormous historical distance—but in many other respects "it breaks free and mocks [our] human attempts to contain it in this simple [historical] category" (Carnley, 94). Rowan Williams, a former archbishop of Canterbury, while conceding a certain "objectivity" to the accounts of the resurrection, acknowledges that "it is not a straightforward matter to say what the gospels understand by the resurrection of Jesus: but it must have something to do with the fact that the Christian communities of the last quarter of the first Christian century didn't find it all that straightforward either" (On

Christian Theology, 187).

The Gospel accounts offer a very believable picture of the imme-
diate experience of the disciples when faced with the risen Jesus. All
testify to the fear and amazement at the shock of encountering something utterly beyond anything they might have anticipated and clearly
confronting the limitations of language. The resurrection is a unique,
revelatory, and redemptive interruption into how things are. Because
of this event, so the New Testament claims, everything is different—we
inhabit an entirely new reality. "So if anyone is in Christ, there is a new
creation: everything old has passed away; see, everything has become
new!" (2 Cor 5:17). Some people claim that it does not really matter
whether this event really happened, all that matters is a resurrection
faith that will generate the possibility of living in a new kind of way.
But the Christian Scriptures are clear: the resurrection is the very
source of faith, and that faith is the very response to the resurrection.

Catholic theologian James Alison asserts that "We have faith at
all because we receive a witness" (Alison, *Knowing Jesus*, 5). The narratives concerning the resurrection indicate that something had clearly
happened to Jesus and, as a result, something had clearly happened to
them. The Gospels are witness to the apostolic experience of resurrection: the result of such experience is a re-visioning of their experience
of the last few years prior to the resurrection. Former archbishop of
Canterbury Michael Ramsey makes this abundantly clear:

"The earthly ministry [of Jesus of Nazareth] was remembered,
handed down and taught never as a self-contained biography, always
as a part of the Gospel of God whose climax is the Passion and the
Resurrection. The words and deeds of Jesus were narrated with the
light of the Resurrection upon them. For the first Christians lived in
a double perspective: the risen Jesus at the right hand of God and the
Jesus of Galilee and Jerusalem" (Ramsey, *Resurrection of Christ*, 12).

In the first place, the writers of the Christian Scriptures are witnesses to the resurrection, witnesses not just of a historical event that
happened in the past but of a transformative and saving reality in the

present. At the same time, the writers are witnesses *from* the resurrection. Alison says the resurrection "was a happening which profoundly changed them, not only turning pusillanimous fisher-folk into international heroes and martyrs but causing them to rethink the whole of their lives, their relationship with their homeland, their culture, its values, and radically altering their understanding of who God is" (Alison, *Knowing Jesus*, 7).

The Gospels are clear: if we want to know about the resurrection and experience it, we will have to stop thinking about it and live it. Mark's Gospel ends abruptly. It does not include any resurrection appearances, offering us not an answer but rather an ongoing question, a question that keeps on asking of us a response, a response that means taking the next step. This is the life and risk of faith, the commitment and following that is called discipleship. This is crucial in our understanding of the resurrection. What difference does belief in the resurrection make in our lives, what implications does it have for us in our everyday life, how does it change our world, and how do we then participate in this new creation? All this is grist for the mill in the practice of spiritual direction, whose orientation is not doctrinal orthodoxy, rather, living life congruently and with integrity. No wonder American poet and ecologist Wendell Berry ended one of his poems with the words "Practice Resurrection" (Berry, 151–52). Practicing resurrection suggests a shift from head to heart and hands.

New Testament scholar Luke Timothy Johnson makes a useful distinction concerning practice: "It is better to speak of 'learning Jesus' than of 'Knowing Jesus' [for] we are concerned with a process rather than a product" (Johnson, 57). This process involves a creative fidelity and implies reciprocity, respect, openness, silence, reflection, patience, and suffering, all dispositions that the ministry of spiritual direction wishes to encourage. The questions remain—they will always remain. They can remain as obstacles, denying us the reality of new life, or, in some miracle of exchange, they can open us up towards the promise of Galilee. And this often happens through the ministry of spiritual direction and the prayer, silence, and waiting that undergird such a ministry.

the old questions lie
folded and in a place
by themselves, like the piled
graveclothes of love's risen body.

—Thomas (359)

If the resurrection is the source and substance of the new life we have in Christ, then surely it is at the very heart of Christian spiritual direction. It is not something we can see or understand directly; but by its light, we see everything else. At least, in the first place, the spiritual director is someone whose whole life is founded upon the reality of the resurrection: her very person finds meaning and purpose in the risen Christ and will inform her life and ministry. Crucially, she will be a witness from the resurrection, and this will be her lived experience. If this is not the case, in Paul's words, her "faith is futile." As she makes space for the "other" who is coming to her for spiritual direction, she is preparing a place for a possible encounter with the risen Christ.

Australian theologian Peter Carnley says, "The Easter stories are not for the purpose of reporting the Easter event in literal detail but they are told and re-told for the purpose of alerting the hearer to a possibility of present experience: their religious purpose lies in their ability to arouse astonishment and thoughtfulness, to turn us around and direct our attention to the eschatological reality of the presence of Christ in our midst" (Carnley, 367). The fact that the historicity of these stories of the appearances of the risen Jesus cannot be resolved need not be an occasion for regret but rather an encouragement for us to see in our puzzlement a gift, directing our attention and alerting us to the possibility of a living encounter with the Risen One. The theological truth these stories offer us is a truth that is not propositional but a truth of a dispositional kind, preparing us for a genuine encounter (Carnley, 364).

Thinking about the ministry of the spiritual director in these terms, offering space for people to grow dispositionally, and in some way learning to empty ourselves to increase our receptive capacity, provides a wonderful stance with which to attend to the stories concerning the appearances of the risen Jesus. Nineteenth-century spiritual director Baron von Hügel suggests that "dispositions are the means to acquiring reality" (Hügel, 14). It is precisely here, where we are, that we wake up to the real presence of the risen Christ, not in doctrinal formula but "in the warmth and sweetness and dryness and terror of actual living" (Williams, *Joy of God*, 24). In other words, we are to inhabit our reality.

People do not come to spiritual direction because the director has some personal wisdom or special illumination from God to pass on. The spiritual director knows, only too well, that she has no solution at hand, for "the answer lies within us ... given to us in advance, in the inmost part of our being, by the Spirit of God given to us" (Louf, 103). This should not surprise us, for "God is always in some mysterious way involved in the complex tangle of desires and fears" in our own lives, and this is precisely the place where God is waiting to reveal Godself to us (Louf, 103). The spiritual director is not there to break down whatever it is that hides this tangle from us: simply, she is there to offer us the room and the place where we ourselves wake up to the encounter that God is wanting for us. The space the spiritual director offers someone coming for spiritual direction arises out of the director's lived experience of "self-emptying." Such "poverty of Spirit" is primarily the disposition that enables the spiritual directee the opportunity of experiencing an "event of the Spirit."

Christ the Stranger

Christ was rarely recognized by sight.

They had to get beyond the way he looked.
Evidence stronger than his voice and face and footstep
Waited to grow in them, to guide their groping
Out of despair, their stretching toward belief.

— Shaw (154)

The resurrection narratives are strange stories about a stranger who is strangely alive. They consistently tell of the trauma, shock, and dislocation the disciples experienced after the crucifixion. Jesus himself condemns their inadequate understanding of who he really is. He is clearly not what they thought he was, and these same stories indicate their slow coming to terms with the new reality brought about by the resurrection. It is as if they must start all over again.

In John's account, Jesus appears to the disciples by the Sea of Tiberius, "but they did not know it was Jesus" (Jn 21:4). This theme of not recognizing Jesus, accompanied by fear, grief, doubt, and even joy, is repeated again and again in the appearance stories. Mary Magdalene stands outside the tomb weeping, and she tells the angels that she does not know where Jesus has been laid. She turns and sees Jesus, "but she did not know that it was Jesus" and supposed him to be the gardener. It was only after Jesus had said to her "Mary!" (Jn 20:11–18) that she knew not only who he was but also who she was—love breaks in, and in being addressed, she finds herself both named and called and changed forever. In Luke's account of the two disciples "going to a village called Emmaus," Jesus "came near and went with them, but their eyes were kept from recognizing him." Cleopas, one of the two, said to Jesus, "Are you the only stranger in Jerusalem who does not know the things that have taken place?" They were sad: "We had hoped," they said, and we cannot escape the depth and longing in those words. And Jesus said, "How foolish and slow of heart to believe all that the prophets had declared," but when he stayed with them and broke bread, "their eyes were opened" (Lk 24:13–35).

In the telling of the story, the one coming for direction will possibly resist or come to an inner truth only by a circuitous and surprising route, speaking of dashed hopes, disappointment, and false expectations. The process of awakening takes time, it cannot be forced. And we must "tell all the truth," as poet Emily Dickinson wrote, "but tell it slant—/Success in Circuit lies" (Dickinson, No. 1263). The disciples on the road to Emmaus told their truth, however disappointing, and it was only on reflection, after the breaking of the bread with the stranger, that they could exclaim, "Did not our hearts burn within us?" (Luke 24:32).

The resurrection is described in confusing, unsettling, and even contradictory ways, and it clearly transcends what we normally understand as history, language, and knowledge. It calls for a radical reorientation of how we think about God, ourselves, and life itself. Christ comes to us often disguised as a stranger, through the events, circumstances, and relationships that happen to us. So much of the work of spiritual direction focuses around at once the "givenness," the unexpected, and the strangeness of otherness. Though it is important to note that "the other is not the obstacle in the way of my coming-to be, but is what makes my coming-to-be possible" (Alison, *Undergoing God*, 118). Of course, the good news of Christ is that he really comes as friend, offering comfort, familiarity, and assurance. But a friend is often too close or familiar for us to see clearly and objectively. Christ as stranger means that the Divine can never be in our grasp nor a projection, speaking about our need rather than what God continually offers. In many ways, Christ as stranger offers us the insight that we are, too often, strangers to ourselves, and the way forward to new life will always be through the acceptance of our own strangeness.

> *Give back your heart to itself,*
> *to the stranger who has loved you*
> *all your life, whom you ignored*

for another, who knows you by heart.

—Walcott (*Love after Love*, 182)

The dialogue that is spiritual direction demands that the director leave the place that is familiar and leave behind her thoughts and feelings so as to inhabit and experience the thoughts and feelings of the other. Such self-emptying will raise questions for the spiritual director: How comfortable am I with difference, with otherness? How tolerant am I of ambiguity, contradiction, and unanswered questions? It is an affirmation and sealing of the truth and glory of the practice of spiritual direction, can I "make space for difference? Can I recognize God's image in someone who is not in my image, whose language, faith, ideals, are different from mine?" (Sacks, 201). However strange or different the other is, can I be present in such a way that this meeting can become an "event of the Spirit"?

Christ the Wound

"Christ's resurrection ... is a wound, a trauma that strikes at the roots of human identity" (Myers, 37). Whatever we might say about the crucifixion and the utter grief and crisis this meant for those disciples, nothing can ever be the same again. The resurrection is not simply a happy ending, a rubbing out of the trauma of death, or a reversal of self-giving love. This was a truth that took time to absorb and accept: "The meaning is in the waiting" (Thomas, 199). The truth about the resurrection remained for the disciples, and remains for us, a completely unexpected and radically new understanding of who God really is, an insight that has the extraordinary capacity to transform our lives. What Jesus did, and what the ministry of spiritual direction affirms, was not that we could deny the reality of everyday life, but that we could continue to realize that resurrection is at the very heart of our worst moments. This is an astonishing and challenging truth that bewilders us, just as it bewildered those first disciples, but it is a truth that leads us in an on-going process of self-discovery. When Jesus said to his disciples before his crucifixion that "those who want to save their life will lose it, and those who lose their life for my sake, and for the sake of the gospel, will save it," (Mk 8:35) he was saying that the process of finding "life-through-death" was not only the truth about God but the truth of their existence and, indeed, the very truth of our humanity.

Thomas says "unless I see the mark of the nails in his hands, and put finger in the mark of the nails, and my hand in his side" he will not believe (Jn 20: 24–29). Thomas was to learn, decisively and overwhelmingly, that we ourselves are part of the mystery that confronts us. While searching for proof "out there," he discovered from within that Jesus's wounds were his own, Jesus' death was his death, and Jesus' life was his own life. Here, Thomas is undone. The objective-subjective continuum collapses, and Thomas, defenseless before God, experiences Meister Eckhart's insight that "The eye with which I see God is exactly the same eye with which God sees me" (Sweeney and Burrows, 210). No wonder Thomas could do nothing other than exclaim, "My Lord and my God." Through a radical de-centering of self, he comes to be centered in a new way in Jesus' own relationship with God, such that, as Paul expresses it, "it is no longer I who live, but it is Christ who lives in me" (Gal 2:20).

Jesus questions Peter three times, matching Peter's three denials: "Do you love me?" Peter felt hurt because Jesus asked him a third time, "Do you love me?" (Jn 21:15–19). Jesus, we might say, is God's question to us. It is a question that wounds—the wound of self-knowledge. God, in Jesus, is a question to which our lives can become an answer. Love always seeks a response of love, and this wounding is nothing less than grace, which is both gift and response. Like both Thomas and Peter, we are radically addressed in the very circumstances of our lives, and the response we make and the actions we take have the capacity to bring meaning and hope to our lives. In this spirit, Australian academic and poet Kevin Hart poignantly ends the poem "The Companion" with the line "I come to wound you and to heal the wound" (Hart, 87).

We live in a visibly untransformed world. It is not obvious that God is in charge. Our world is both wounded and wounding. Each of us carries wounds that are etched in us: memories of betrayals, jealousies, theft, and abuse. These wounds are deeply personal, relational and communal, and societal and global; these wounds arise from our clear-eyed self-deception to form deeply hidden motivations and prejudices. Our woundedness has to do with our incompleteness, our not being in control, and our not knowing. Our knowledge of God is not an assured accomplishment but rather a wounding knowledge of ourselves, poor and dependent.

The spiritual director has the unique gift and opportunity to provide a safe space for someone to begin to acknowledge his vulnerability and woundedness. Such vulnerability is about how we carry our wounds, whether they lead to life or to death. The how in "how we carry our wounds" is a hugely significant word in spiritual direction. It allows a person to move beyond trying harder or feeling guilty, to seeing that whatever he is carrying actually leads somewhere, either towards more entanglement and addiction or freedom, to either living or dying. To wake up to the fact that whatever has brought this situation into expression and focus holds out the possibility of an encounter with the truth that sets us free, leading us from a doctrinally sterile questioning about what happened "back then" to a creative, transformative "event of the Spirit" in the present.

So, the spiritual director is always encouraging the directee to pause on what has been happening in his life—to reflect and listen and savor, to realize that there is really no safe vantage point from where we can speak realistically about God. Places of uncertainty, bewilderment, and even fear can all be places of grace where we are offered opportunities to hear both the question and the invitation towards life. We are often tempted to be in a hurry to fix things up or smooth things over. As English television dramatist Dennis Potter warns in a final interview before his death, "Religion is never the bandage, always the wound" (Rockwell, 1994).

Christ the Forgiving Victim

When Jesus appeared to Paul on the road to Damascus, Paul asked, "Who are you, Lord?" He replied, "I am Jesus, whom you are persecuting" (Acts 9:5). The Jesus who appeared to Paul was not the triumphant or victorious one but rather the persecuted one. As the risen One, he still bears the marks of crucifixion. The church, those Christians whom Saul has been persecuting, the very body of Jesus, the presence of God, and nothing less than unconditional forgiveness. This turns him completely around. Here is the possibility of an entirely new life, a radical reordering of everything he has ever believed. Jesus stands before him—and us—not as accusation but as forgiveness. The objects of his persecution—the early Christians—are none other than Christ's body, the gratuitous presence of a forgiving God. It is as if Paul is undone: "The body we killed is the body we are in" (Moore, 48–49). This transition, from the body dead to the body alive, occurs with almost overwhelming consequences, when we hear again the angel's question: "Why do you look for the living among the dead?" (Lk 24:5). "The now" in experiencing the resurrection is the now of feeling ourselves as a new community. What seemed like something that occurred "out there" (or for us "back then"), puzzling our minds, is suddenly something that happens "in here," from within.

Standing before Christ as the "forgiving victim" (Alison, *Knowing Jesus*, 37) is a deeply personal, deeply intimate, and deeply self-implicating experience. Letting him look at us in all our nakedness is disarming and unsettling. Sharing something of this experience with a spiritual director suggests at least that this is an astonishingly relational and communal event. This is no mere external transaction; this strikes at the very heart of what it means to be human and what it means to be me. Our mind, let alone our whole being, can fathom neither what is happening nor its meaning.

That we are part of the very mystery that we are seeking and longing to understand is the crucial breakthrough needed. The spiritual director stands with those coming to her in solidarity; it is her poverty that provides the healing sanctuary and space for the other. The apostolic witnesses and their hearers are neither neutral nor innocent, nor are they simply giving us information. They are involved and implicated in Jesus's death. The preaching of the resurrection is not addressed to an abstract audience; the victim at the center of this story is the victim of the hearers. Each of us is human, and each of us is both victim and maker of victims. The risen Christ confronts us with this fact. It is a confrontation that is both shattering and healing, reducing us to a poverty we find hard to accept, yet a poverty that is utterly transforming. "The resurrection is forgiveness: not a decree about forgiveness, but the presence of gratuity as a person" (Alison, *Knowing Jesus*, 16). Forgiveness is not just about the past; it is also about the future, and it is always about transformation and discipleship. It strikes at the very heart of present life, but it does reveal to us just how crucial to the shaping of our lives the future vision of the kingdom really is. But the language of Jesus about the kingdom is also crucially about a present reality—and it is the same language as Paul's language about the resurrection (Paul being the earliest written witness to the resurrection).

The language of the kingdom has become the language of the resurrection. The empty tomb and the appearance stories can now be seen as interpreting Jesus's resurrection as the dawning of a totally new creation. Resurrection carries with it an immense meaning, but only when we live it and cooperate with it, so that it energizes us to work towards making the world more just. The nuclear explosion, which is the resurrection, means that forgiveness means both being forgiven and forgiving. The revolution that upturned the disciples' lives, and can overturn ours, is that the risen Christ's life is our life, his truth the very truth of our existence. So, the resurrection is no mere theoretical or philosophical vision of human destiny: it is a charter for action, for belief in the resurrection carries within it an inner dynamic that is both transformative and liberating.

New Testament scholar N. T. Wright succinctly states, "[The gospels] say that Jesus is raised, therefore God's new creation has begun, and we've got a job to do" (Stewart, 21). Therefore, the spiritual director is alert to the secret of the resurrection life: it is not about proving that something happened back then, nor is it simply contained in a person's subjective experience. We have a job to do, and the spiritual director waits attentively for the possible transition in the directee from self-concern towards another. This fundamental orientation towards the other is our truth—the truth about humanity—and it is at the same time the truth about God. The resurrection is always about falling in love—moving from self towards the other—and such faithfulness to our in-built capacity for self-transcendence will always lead towards a genuinely objective experience of the new creation.

The Absent Christ

He is such a fast
God, always before us and
Leaving as we arrive.

—Thomas (364)

One of Canadian novelist Anne Michaels' characters says, "How do we know there's a God? Because He keeps disappearing" (Michaels, 107). If Christ as stranger disconcerts us, and Christ as wound and forgiving victim confronts us, Christ as absence both confounds and disappoints us—Christ is always just beyond our grasp, always going before us to Galilee. Since the time of the resurrection, when the angel's message was "He is not here. He is risen," (Lk 24:5) we have clung to our idea of God, but as C. S. Lewis pointed out, our idea of God "has to be shattered time after time. He shatters it Himself. He is the great iconoclast. Could we not almost say that this shattering is one of the marks of His presence?" (Lewis, 55–56). The resurrection is the shattering, life-changing revolution we need to wake up to the mysterious, ungraspable fact that our future is breaking into our present. That future has already appeared in Christ. If we can purge ourselves of all the ideas, thoughts, and images we hang onto and recognize our utter dependency and poverty before God, we can begin to realize that it is here, in the experience of our lowliness before the Creator, where we are touched by the life of the new creation.

The challenge of the risen Jesus is that he is utterly free—free from local limitation, free from the limitations of the past, free from our projections and expectations, and free from our neediness and wants. "Do not hold me" says that he is, and always must be, beyond our grasp. This is strange territory for us (Jn 20:17). We struggle to find the right words for such an unfamiliar experience. But resurrection is the journey through deception into truth, through unreality into reality, and through illusion and falsehood into freedom; the ministry of spiritual direction offers us encouragement as we face such imaginative and conceptual poverty. In the presence of the risen Jesus, we will have to leave thought and speech behind and enter the silence of not knowing. "The dawn breaks [only] when we have entered fully into the night" (R. Williams, *Open*, 99). What the early Christians slowly came to see is that the very character of God is seen in Christ's moment of dereliction, when Jesus cries from the cross, "My God, my God, why have you forsaken me?" (Mk 15:34) here is "someone who understands you completely, who is with you in your cry to God and has felt the same forsakenness you are living in now" (Moltmann, 30).

The empty tomb is the most potent symbol of Christ's absence, yet paradoxically, it is the most liberating symbol of his presence. It symbolizes the presence of God more eloquently and accurately than any human words or actions could shape. God hides from us to prevent us from thinking we can grasp or even comprehend God. Such absence or hiddenness draws us into the endless search for God, which is the human condition—this search for the ungraspable that mysteriously grasps us. The person coming for direction may be surprised and disoriented at the new situation he finds himself in. Life, hitherto, while having its usual ups and downs, was at least fairly predictable. But a crisis, a big decision, or a drastic change in circumstances has broken him free of the usual dependencies and left a void—a wound that cries out for healing. The diagnosis that Jesus makes of the human condition is that we cannot see, and even when we can see, our vision is either distorted or inadequate. We fear this truth about ourselves, but it can become the place where we confront our prejudices, blind spots, projections, and illusions, and it can liberate us and transform us into what Paul would call "the new creation."

The ministry of spiritual direction is a ministry where we can accompany others on a journey of awakening and recognition. When Jesus said to the disciples, who had gone fishing, to "Cast the net to the right side of the boat, and you will find some" (Jn 21:6), he was suggesting that it was possible to find another perspective, another way of looking at things. Recognizing that we cannot see, or that we cannot see properly, requires courage and patience and space. This is the space God clears for us in Jesus, who makes it possible for us to live where he lives, the place where God and human reality coexist. The new life on offer, in this spaciousness of God that we find in Jesus, "is not a possession. It is, simply, new life—a new world of possibilities and a new future that is to be constructed day by day. Life, after all, implies movement and growth" (Williams, *Wound of Knowledge*, 8). The primary invitations for the spiritual director are to stay out of the way, to be a safe and loving presence, and to be so encouraging and careful and patient that a space is created for both director and directee. In this space, a spiritual director can listen a person into speech and look a person into life, so that it truly becomes a place of transfiguration, whereby "we bring the total situation as we ourselves participate in it, into a larger context which gives it new meaning" (Ramsey quoting C.

H. Dodd, *The Glory of God*, 146). Waiting patiently with another, in the face of a silent and hidden God, is the very heart of spiritual direction. This is no opportunity for teaching or preaching but rather for waiting—waiting in this space where a very human reality and the goodness and love of God are allowed to belong together. Holding these two together for the sake of another is the marvel, the mystery, and the miracle of spiritual direction.

REFERENCES

Allchin, A. M. *The World Is a Wedding: Explorations in Christian Spirituality*. London: Darton, Longman and Todd, 1978.

Alison, James. *Knowing Jesus*. New ed. London: Society for Promoting Christian Knowledge, 1998.

———. *Undergoing God: Dispatches from the Scene of a Break-in*. New York: Continuum, 2006.

Andrewes, Lancelot. *Complete Works*. Vol. 3. Edited by the Library of Anglo-Catholic Theology.

Arendt, Hannah. *The Human Condition*. Garden City, NY: Doubleday Anchor Book, 1958.

Arrupe. "The Man Who Was There." Seattle University. https://www.seattleu.speeches-and-homilies.

Auden, W. H. *Collected Shorter Poems: 1927–1957*. London: Faber & Faber, 1976, 1994.

———. *For the Time Being: A Christmas Oratorio*. Princeton, NJ: Princeton University Press, 2013.

Bachelard, Sarah. *Experiencing God in a Time of Crisis*. Miami, FL: Convivium Press, 2012.

———. *Resurrection and Moral Imagination*. London: Routledge, 2016.

Baker, John Austin. *The Foolishness of God*. London: Darton, Longman

& Todd Ltd. 1970.

Balthasar, Hans Urs von. *Prayer*. London: SPCK, 1961.

Barry, S.J., William A. *Paying Attention to God*. Notre Dame, Indiana: Ave Maria Press, 1990, 126.

Beckett, Sister Wendy. *The Mystery of Love: Saints in Art through the Centuries*. London: HarperCollins, 1996.

Benedict XVI. *Deus Caritas Est*. Sydney: Saint Paul's Publications, 2006.

Bernanos, Georges. *The Diary of a Country Priest*. London: Catholic Book Club, 1937.

Berry, Wendell. *Collected Poems, 1957–1982*. San Francisco: North Point Press, 1985.

————. *This Day: Collected and New Sabbath Poems*. Berkeley, CA: Counterpoint, 2013.

Bonhoeffer, Dietrich. *The Cost of Discipleship*. Rev. ed. London: SCM Press, 1959.

————. *Letters and Papers from Prison*. Edited by Eberhard Bethge. London: Collins, Fontana Books, 1959.

————. *Prayers from Prison: Prayers and Poems*. Translated by Johann Christoph Hampe. Philadelphia: Fortress Press, 1978.

Bourgeault, Cynthia. *Centering Prayer and Inner Awakening*. Plymouth, UK: Cowley Publications, 2004.

Buechner, Frederick. *Wishful Thinking: A Theological ABC.* London: Harper & Row, 1973.

Campbell, Alastair. *Rediscovering Pastoral Care.* London: Darton, Longman, and Todd, 1981.

Carnley, Peter. *The Structure of Resurrection Belief.* Oxford: Clarendon Press, 1987.

Casey, Michael. *Fully Human, Fully Divine: An Interactive Christology.* Mulgrave, Victoria, Australia: John Garratt Publishing, 2004.

Chesterton, G. K. *St. Francis of Assisi.* London: Hodder & Stoughton, 1923.

————. *Autobiography.* London: Burns & Oates, 1937.

Clément, Olivier. *The Roots of Christian Mysticism: Texts from the Patristic Era with Commentary.* New York: New City Press, 1995.

Cox, Harvey. *The Future of Faith.* New York: HarperCollins, 2009.

Delio, Ilia. *The Emergent Christ: Exploring the Meaning of Catholic in an Evolutionary Universe.* Maryknoll, NY: Orbis Books, 2011.

Dessaix, Robert. *Corfu: A Novel.* London: Simon & Schuster, 2003.

Denniston, Robin. *Trevor Huddleston: A Life.* London: Macmillan Pan Books, 2000.

Dickinson, Emily. *The Poems of Emily Dickinson.* Edited by R. W. Franklin. Cambridge, MA: Belknap Press of Harvard University Press, 2005.

Ecclestone, Alan. *Yes to God*. London: Darton, Longman & Todd, 1975.

———. *A Staircase for Silence*. London: Darton, Longman and Todd, 1977.

———. *The Scaffolding of Spirit: Reflections on the Gospel of St. John*. London: Darton, Longman and Todd, 1987.

Edwards, Denis. *Breath of Life: A Theology of the Creator Spirit*. New York: Orbis Books, 2004.

Eliot, T. S. "Burnt Norton." *Four Quartets: A Poem*. London: Faber & Faber, 1959.

———. *Four Quartets*. London: Faber and Faber, 1959.

———. *The Complete Poems and Plays of T. S. Eliot*. London: Faber and Faber, 1969.

Elliott, Charles. *Praying the Kingdom: Towards a Political Spirituality*. London: Darton, Longman and Todd, 1985.

Enright, D. J., and Ernst de Chickera, eds. *English Critical Texts: 16th Century to 20th Century*. London: Oxford University Press, 1962.

Finley, James. *Merton's Palace of Nowhere: A Search for God through Awareness of the True Self*. Notre Dame, IN: Ave Maria Press, 1978.

Fischer, Kathleen. *The Inner Rainbow: The Imagination in Christian Life*. New York: Paulist Press, 1983.

Fleming, David L. *Draw Me Into your Friendship: A Literal Translation and a Contemporary Reading of the Spiritual Exercises*. St. Louis: Institute of Jesuit Sources, 1996.

Ford, David F. *The Shape of Living: The Spiritual Directions for Everyday Life*. London: HarperCollins Fontana, 1997.

Furlong, Monica. *God's a Good Man and Other Poems*. London: Mowbrays, 1974.

Galilea, Segundo. *Following Jesus*. Maryknoll, NY: Orbis Books, 1985.

Gallagher, Michael Paul. *Free to Believe: Ten Steps to Faith*. London: Darton, Longman & Todd, 1985.

———. *Dive Deeper: The Human Poetry of Faith*. London: Darton, Longman & Todd, 2001.

———. "The Peak of Our Freedom: Bernard Lonergan for Today." *Spirituality 15* (Sept.-Oct. 2009): 316.

Gilkey, Langdon. *Naming the Whirlwind: The Renewal of God-language*. Indianapolis: Bobbs-Merrill, 1969.

Guenther, Margaret. *Holy Listening: The Art of Spiritual Direction*. London: Darton, Longman and Todd, 1992.

Gratton, Carolyn. *Guidelines for Spiritual Direction*. Denville, NJ: Dimension Books, 1980.

———. *The Art of Spiritual Guidance: A Contemporary Approach to Growing in the Spirit*. New York: Crossroad, 1993.

Grün, Anselm. *Images of Jesus*. London: Continuum, 2002.

Hammarskjöld. *Markings*. Translated by W. H. Auden and Leif Sjöberg. London: Faber & Faber, 1964.

Heschel, Abraham Joshua. *God in Search of Man: A Philosophy of Judaism*. New York: Farrar, Straus and. New York, 1978.

Hart, Kevin. *New & Selected Poems*. Sydney: Angus & Robertson, 1995.

Havel, Václav. *Letters to Olga*. London: Faber and Faber, 1988.

Hillesum, Etty. *Etty: A Diary, 1941–1943*. London: Triad, 1985.

Huddleston, C.R., Trevor. *Naught for Your Comfort*. London: Collins, 1956.

Hügel, Friedrich von. *Letters to a Niece*. London: J. M. Dent & Sons Ltd., 1928.

Hughes, Gerard. *God of Surprises*. London: Darton, Longman and Todd, 1985.

Illich, Ivan. *Celebration of Awareness: A Call for Institutional Revolution*. Harmondsworth, UK: Penguin Books, 1973.

Jennings, Elizabeth. *Selected Poems*. Manchester, UK: Carcanet, 1986.

John, Jeffrey, ed. *Living Tradition: Affirming Catholicism in the Anglican Church*. London: Darton, Longman and Todd,1992.

John Paul II, Pope. *Ut Unum Sint: Encylical Letter of the Holy Father John Paul II on Commitment to Ecumenism*. Boston: Pauline Books and Media, 1995.

Johnson, Elizabeth. *She Who Is: The Mystery of God in Feminist Theological Discourse*. New York: Crossroad, 1992.

————. *Friends of God and Prophets: A Feminist Theological Reading of the Communion of Saints*. New York: Continuum, 1998.

Johnson, Luke Timothy. *Living Jesus: Learning the Heart of the Gospel*. New York: HarperCollins, 2000.

Jones, Alan. *Exploring Spiritual Direction: An Essay in Christian Friendship*. New York: Seabury Press, 1982.

————. *Soul Making: The Desert Way of Spirituality*. London: SCM Press, 1985.

Julian of Norwich. *Showings*. Translated by Edmund Colledge and James Walsh. New York: Paulist Press, 1978.

————. *Revelations of Divine Love*. Translated by Elizabeth Spearing. London: Penguin Books, 1998.

Keen, Sam. *The Passionate Life: Stages of Loving*. San Francisco: Harper & Row, 1983.

Lane, Dermot. *The Experience of God: An Invitation to Do Theology*. New York: Paulist Press, 1981.

Lee, Dorothy. *Transfiguration*. London: Continuum, 2004.

Leunig, Michael. *A Common Prayer*. Melbourne: Harper Collins, 1990.

Levertov, Denise. *New Selected Poems*. Northumberland, UK: Bloodaxe Books, 2003.

Lewis, C. S. *A Grief Observed*. London: Faber and Faber, (1961) 1987.

Lewis, C. S., and Walter Hooper. *The Business of Heaven: Daily Readings from C. S. Lewis* ed. by Walter Hooper. London: Fount, 1991, 22.

Lossky, Vladimir. *The Mystical Theology of the Eastern Church*. London: James Clarke & Co., 1944, 1957.

Louf, André. *Teach Us to Pray: Learning a Little about God*. London: Darton, Longman & Todd, 1974.

————. *Tuning into Grace: The Quest for God*. London: Darton, Longman and Todd, 1992.

Maalouf, Amin. *On Identity*. Translated by Barbara Bray. London: Harvill, 2000.

Mackay, Hugh. *What Makes Us Tick?: The Ten Desires That Drive Us*. Sydney: Hachette Australia, 2010.

McCarty, Shaun. "On Entering Spiritual Direction," in *Spiritual Direction: Contemporary Readings*. Edited by Kevin G. Culligan. Locust Valley, NY: Living Flame Press, 1983.

McEwan, Ian. "At home with his worries." *The Guardian*, September 16, 2001.

McGrandle, Piers. *Trevor Huddleston: Turbulent Priest*. London: Continuum Books, 2004.

Mendonça, José Tolentino. *Our Father, Who Art on Earth*. Adelaide, Australia: ATF Press, 2014.

Merton, Thomas. *New Seeds of Contemplation*. New York: New Directions, 1962.

————. *Conjectures of a Guilty Bystander*. New York: Image Books, 1968.

————. *Contemplative Prayer*, Image Books, Doubleday & Company, Inc., New York,1971, 102.

————. *The Asian Journal of Thomas Merton*. Edited by Patrick Hart, James Laughlin, and Naomi Burton Stone. New York: A New Directions Book, 1975.

————. *Hagia Sophia: The Collected Poems of Thomas Merton*. New York: New Directions, 1977.

————. *Learning to Love: The Journals of Thomas Merton, Volume 6: 1966–1967*. San Francisco, CA: Harper San Francisco, 1997.

————. *Contemplation in a World of Action*. Notre Dame, IN: University of Notre Dame Press, 1998.

Metz, Johannes Baptist. *Poverty of Spirit*. New York: Paulist Press, 1968.

Michaels, Anne. *Fugitive Pieces*. London: Bloomsbury, 1997.

Moltmann, Jürgen. *The Trinity and the Kingdom of God: The Doctrine of God*. London: SCM Press, 1981.

————. *The Crucified God*. London: SCM Press, 1974.

————. *A Broad Place: An Autobiography*. London: SCM Press, 2007.

Moore, Sebastian. *The Fire and the Rose are One*. London: Darton,

Longman & Todd, 1980.

————. *The Contagion of Jesus: Doing Theology as If It Mattered*. London: Darton, Longman and Todd, 2007.

Morwood, Michael. *Praying a New Story*. Melbourne: Spectrum Publications, 2003.

Muir, Edwin. *Collected Poems, 1921–1958*. London: Faber and Faber, 1960.

Murdoch, Iris. "The Sublime and the Good." *Chicago Review* 13, no. 3 (Autumn 1959): 42–55.

Myers, Benjamin. *Christ the Stranger: The Theology of Rowan Williams, a Critical Introduction*. London: Continuum, 2012.

Nouwen, Henri. *The Way of the Heart: Desert Spirituality and Contemporary Ministry*. London: Darton, Longman and Todd, 1981.

O'Driscoll, Dennis, ed. *The Bloodaxe Book of Poetry Quotations*. Northumberland, UK: Bloodaxe Books, 2006.

O'Leary, Daniel. *Begin with the Heart: Recovering a Sacramental Vision*. Dublin: Columbia Press, 2008.

Oliver, Mary. *Dream Work*. Boston: Atlantic Monthly Press, 1986.

————. *Thirst*. Boston: Beacon Press, 2006.

————. *Wild Geese: Selected Poems*. Tarset, England: Bloodaxe Books, 2006.

Peterson, Eugene H. *The Contemplative Pastor: Returning to the Art of*

Spiritual Direction. Grand Rapids, MI: William B. Eerdmans, 1993.

Piercy, Marge. *Circles on the Water: Selected Poems of Marge Piercy.* New York: Knopf, 1982.

Pope Paul VI. *Ecclesiam Suam.* Washington, DC: National Catholic Welfare Conference, 1964.

Potter, Dennis. *Seeing the Blossom: Two Interviews and a Lecture.* London: Faber and Faber, 1994.

Rahner, Karl. *Theological Investigations, Vol. III.* Translated by Karl H. Kruger & Boniface Kruger. London: Darton, Longman and Todd, 1967.

Ramsey, A. M. *The Resurrection of Christ: An Essay in Biblical Theology.* London: Geoffrey Bles, 1945.

————. *The Glory of God and the Transfiguration of Christ.* London: Darton, Longman and Todd, (1949) 1967.

Rich, Adrienne. *The Dream of a Common Language: Poems, 1974–1977.* New York: W. W. Norton, 1978.

Rilke, Rainer Maria. *Letters to a Young Poet.* London: Penguin Books, 2016.

Robinson, John A. T. *The Human Face of God.* London: SCM Press, 1973.

Robinson, Marilynne. *When I Was a Child I Read Books: Essays.* London: Virago Press, 2013.

Rockwell, John. "Dennis Potter's Last Interview, on 'Nowness' and His Work." *The New York Times,* June 12, 1994.

Roethke, Theodore. *Selected Poems*. Edited by Edward Hirsch. London: Faber & Faber, 1969.

Rogers, Carl R. *A Way of Being*. Boston: Houghton Mifflin, 1995.

Rohr, Richard. "Gazing upon the Mystery." *Daily Meditations* (Oct. 21, 2018). Center for Action and Contemplation. https://cac.org/gazing-upon-the-mystery-2018-10-21/.

Rolheiser, Ronald. "Dark Memory." October 16, 1997. https://ronrolheiser.com/dark-memory-2/.

———. *Seeking Spirituality: Guidelines for a Christian Spirituality for the Twenty-First Century*. London: Hodder & Stoughton, 1998.

Ryan, R.S.J., Sr. Gen. "Sight, Insight, Heart Sight, etc." Reflection Paper. Emmaus story workshop.

Sacks, Jonathan. *The Dignity of Difference: How to Avoid a Clash of Civilizations*. Rev. ed. London: Continuum, 2002.

Saint Augustine. *Confessions*. Translated by F. J. Sheed. London: Sheed & Ward, 1944.

———. *The City of God*. New York: The Modern Library, 1950.

Schillebeeckx, Edward. *Jesus: An Experiment in Christology*. London: Collins, 1979.

Schneiders, Sandra M. *Written That You May Believe: Encountering Jesus in the Fourth Gospel*. Rev. ed. New York: Crossroad, 2003.

Schweickart, Russell. "No Frames, No Boundaries." *In Context* no. 3

(Summer 1983): 16–18.

Shaw, Luci. *Polishing the Petoskey Stone: New and Selected Poems*. Wheaton, IL: Harold Shaw, 1990.

Smith, Cyprian. *The Way of Paradox: Spiritual Life as Taught by Meister Eckhart*. London: Darton, Longman and Todd, 1987.

Sobrino, Jon. *Spirituality of Liberation: Toward Political Holiness*. New York: Orbis Books, 1988.

Stewart, Robert B., ed. *The Resurrection of Jesus: John Dominic Crossan and N. T. Wright in Dialogue*. Minneapolis: Fortress Press, 2006.

Suzuki, Shunryu. *Zen Mind, Beginner's Mind*. New York: Weatherhill, 1970.

Sweeney, Jon M., and Mark S. Burrows. *Meister Eckhart's Book of the Heart: Meditations for the Restless Soul*. Charlottesville, VA: Hampton Roads Publishing, 2017.

Tacey, David. *Re-enchantment: The New Australian Spirituality*. Sydney: HarperCollins, 2000.

Taylor, John V. *The Primal Vision: Christian Presence amid African Religion*. London: SCM Press. 1962.

———. *The Go – Between God*. London: SCM Press, 1972.

———. *A Matter of Life and Death*. SCM. London: SCM Press. 1986.

———. *The Christlike God*. London: SCM Press, 1992.

Teilhard de Chardin, Pierre. *Toward the Future.* Translated by René Hague. New York: Harcourt, 1975.

Temple, William. *Readings in St. John's Gospel.* First and second series. London: Macmillan, 1983.

————. *Selected Prose.* Edited by Sandra Anstey. Glamorgan, Wales: Poetry Wales Press, 1983.

Thomas, R. S. *Collected Poems: 1945–1990.* London: Phoenix Giants, 1993.

————. "Emerging." *Collected Poems 1945-1990.* Phoenix Giants, London, 1993.

The transfiguration of Jesus is recorded in the Gospels of Mark 9:2–9, Matthew 17:1–9, and Luke 9:28–36b.

Turner, Denys. *Julian of Norwich, Theologian.* New Haven, CT: Yale University Press, 2011.

————. *Faith Seeking.* London: SCM Press, 2002, 2012.

Tugwell, Simon, O.P. *Reflections on the Beatitudes: Soundings in Christian Traditions.* London: Dalton, Longman and Todd, 1980.

Tutu, Desmond. *God Is Not a Christian: Speaking Truth in Times of Crisis.* London: Rider, 2011.

————. *Believe: The Words and Inspiration of Desmond Tutu.* Sydney, NSW, Australia: Hachette, 2007.

Ulanov, Ann, and Barry Ulanov. *Primary Speech: A Psychology of Prayer.*

Atlanta: John Knox Press, 2007.

Ungunmerr-Baumann, Miriam-Rose. "Dadirri." *Compass Theology Review* 22 (1983):9-11.

Vanstone, W. H. *Love's Endeavour, Love's Expense: The Response of Being to the Love of God.* London: Darton, Longman and Todd: 1977.

———. *Fare Well in Christ.* London: Darton, Longman & Todd, 1997.

———. *The Stature of Waiting.* London: Darton, Longman & Todd, 1997.

Volf, Miroslav. *Exclusion and Embrace: A Theological Exploration of Identity, Otherness, and Reconciliation.* Nashville, TN: Abingdon Press, 1996.

Waal, Esther de. *A Retreat with Thomas Merton: A Seven-Day Spiritual Journey.* Melbourne: John Garratt Publishing, 1992.

———. *Lost in Wonder: Rediscovering the Spiritual Art of Attentiveness.* Mulgrave, Victoria: John Garratt Publishing, 2003.

Walcott, Derek. "Love after Love." In *Being Alive.* 4th ed., edited by Neil Astley Tarset. Northumberland, England: Bloodaxe Books, 2004.

Walsh, James, ed. *The Cloud of Unknowing.* New York: Paulist Press, 1981.

Ward, Sister Benedicta, SLG. *The Wisdom of the Desert Fathers: The "Apophthegmata Patrum" (the Anonymous Series).* Oxford: SLG Press, 1975.

Ware, Kallistos. *The Orthodox Way.* Crestwood, NY: St. Vladimir's Seminary Press, 1979.

Watson, Don. *Death Sentence: The Decay of Public Language*. Sydney: Knopf, 2003.

White, Patrick. *The Solid Mandala*. Harmondsworth, Middlesex, England: Penguin, 1969.

Weil, Simone. *Waiting on God*. London: Fontana Books, 1959.

Whelan, Michael. *Living Strings: An Introduction to Biblical Spirituality*. Sydney: E. J. Dwyer, 1994.

Wilbur, Richard. *Walking to Sleep: New Poems and Translations*. London: Faber and Faber, 1971.

Williams, David-Antoine. "Hesitation, Naming, Poetry," *Poetry and Contingency*. Accessed August 9, 2016. http://poetry-contingency.uwaterloo.ca/ hesitation-naming-poetry/.

Williams, H. A. *The Joy of God: Variations on a Theme*. London: Michael Beazley, 1979.

————. *Some Day I'll Find You*. London: Collins Fount Paperbacks, 1982.

Williams, Rowan. *The Wound of Knowledge: Christian Spirituality from the New Testament to Saint John of the Cross*. London: Darton, Longman and Todd, 1979.

————. "Teaching the Truth." In *Living Tradition: Affirming Catholicism in the Anglican Church*. Edited by Jeffrey John, 29-43. London: Darton, Longman and Todd, 1992.

———. *Open to Judgement: Sermons and Addresses.* London: Darton, Longman and Todd, 1994.

———. *Writing in the Dust: After September 11.* London: Hodder & Stoughton, 2002.

———. *Silence and Honey Cakes: The Wisdom of the Desert.* Oxford: Lion Publishing, 2003.

———. "Space for the divine." *The Tablet,* 26 April, 2008.

———. *Meeting God in Mark: Reflections for the Season of Lent.* London: SPCK, 2014.

———. *What Is Christianity?: A Little Book of Guidance.* London: SPCK Publishing, 2015.

Wilson, A. N. *C. S. Lewis: A Biography.* London: HarperCollins, London, 1991.

Winterson, Jeanette. *Why Be Happy When You Could be Normal?* New York: Grove Press, 2011.

Zeldin, Theodore. *An Intimate History of Humanity.* London: Minerva, 1995.

———. *Conversation: How Talk Can Change Our Lives.* London: Harvill Press, London, 1998.

Made in the USA
Monee, IL
26 November 2024

70577636R00111